Adult Coloring Books
Monstrous Mandalas

Mandala Floral Pattern, Flowers, Paisley, Doodles and Decorative Designs

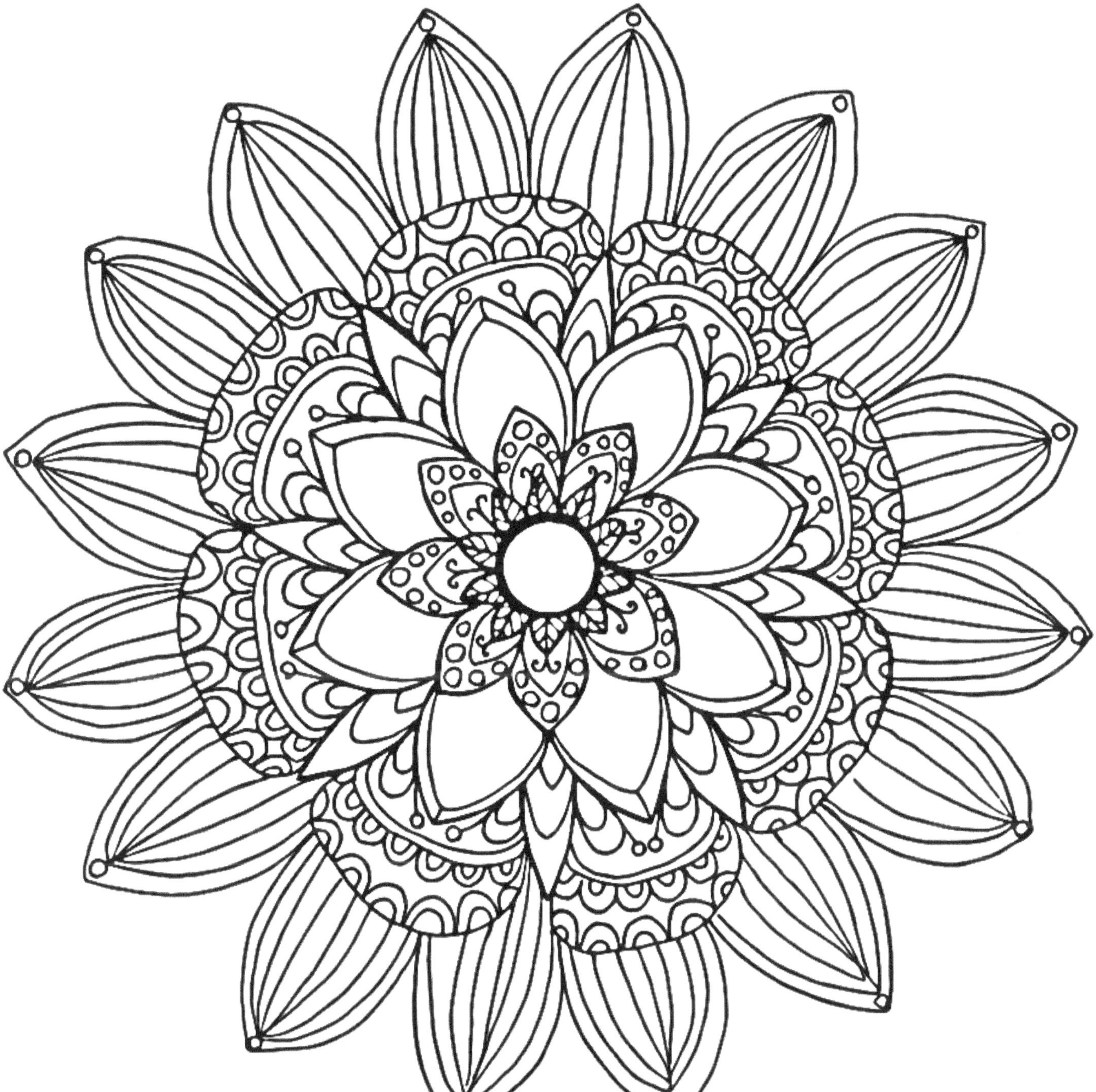

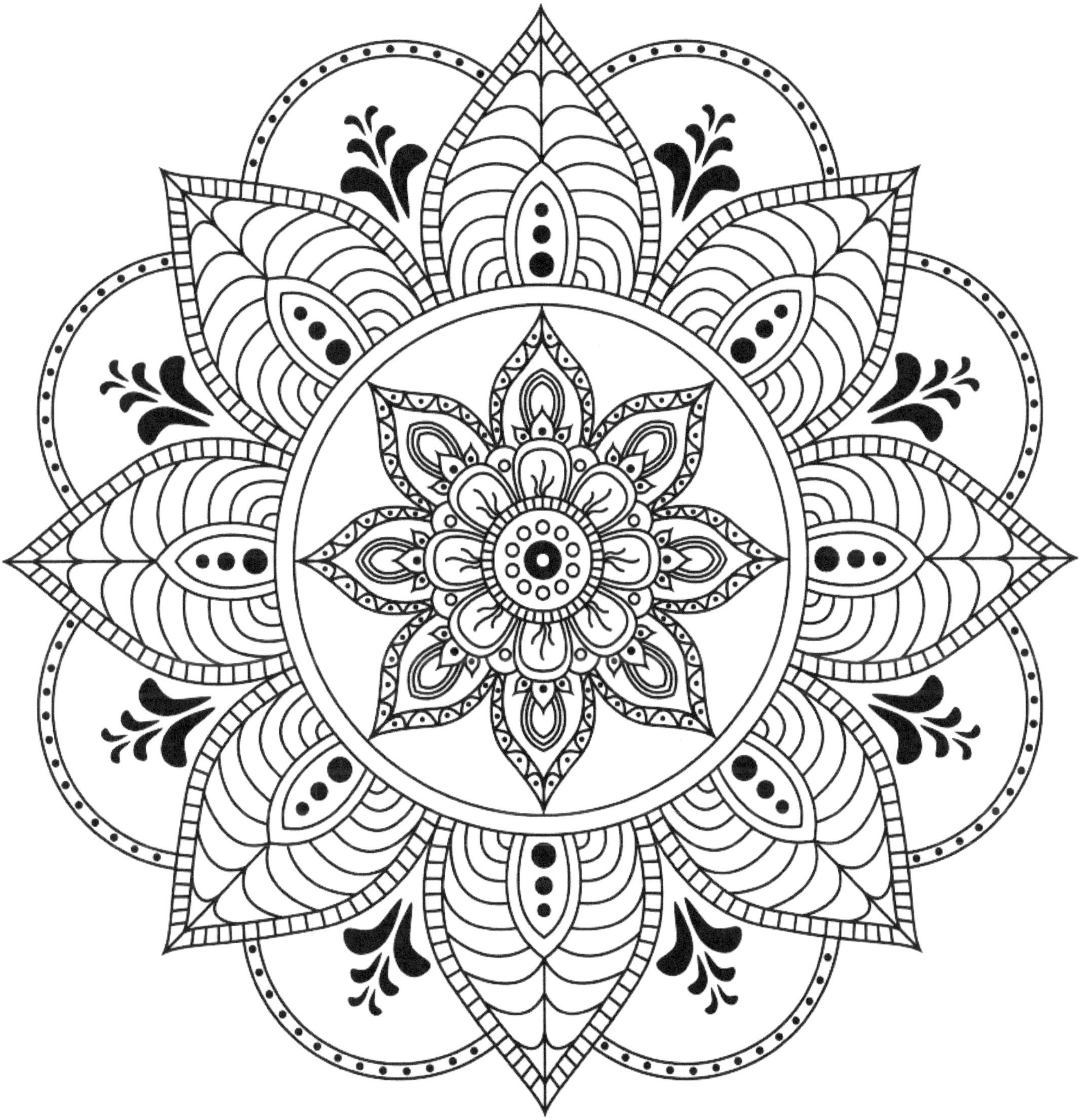

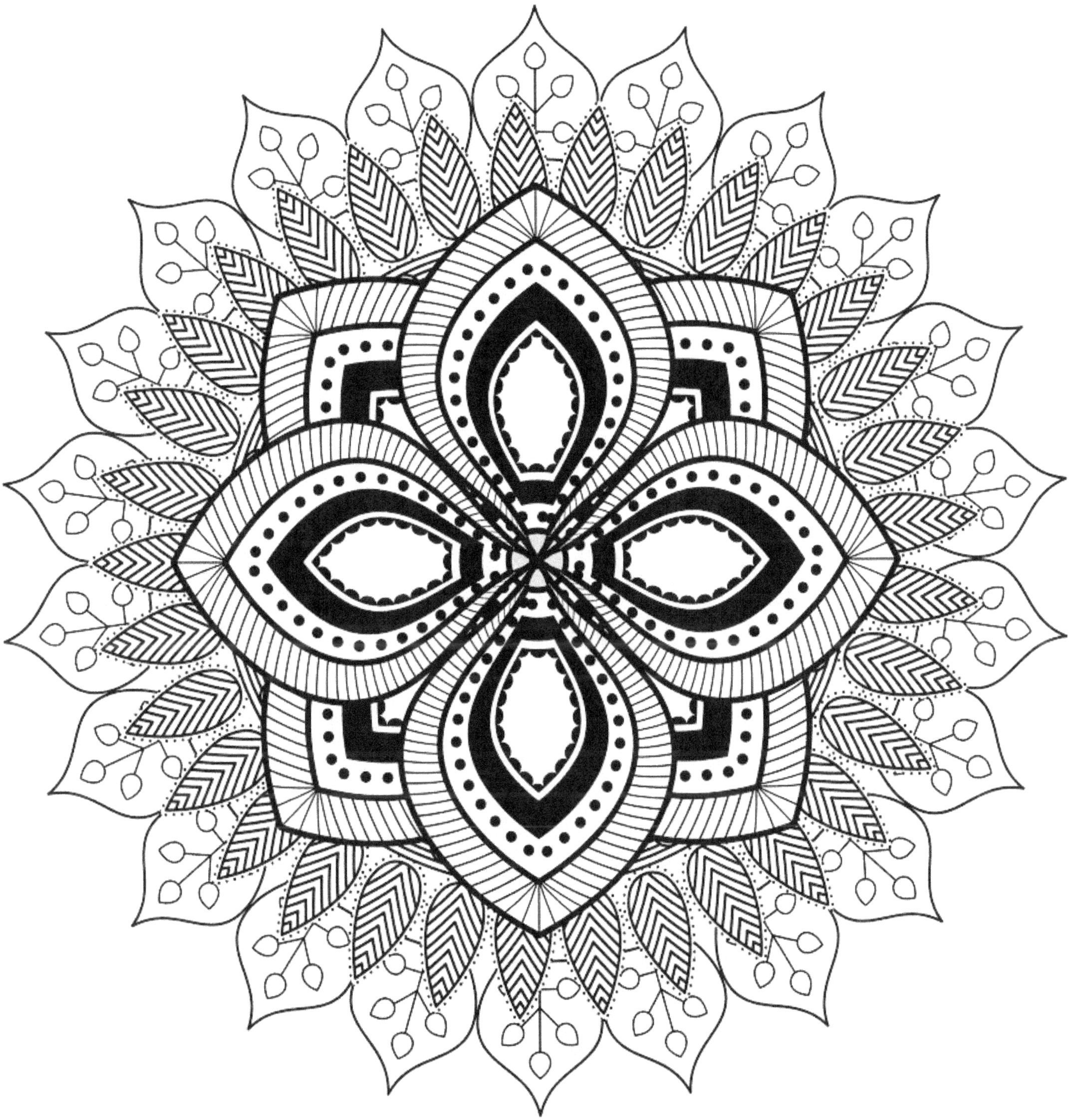

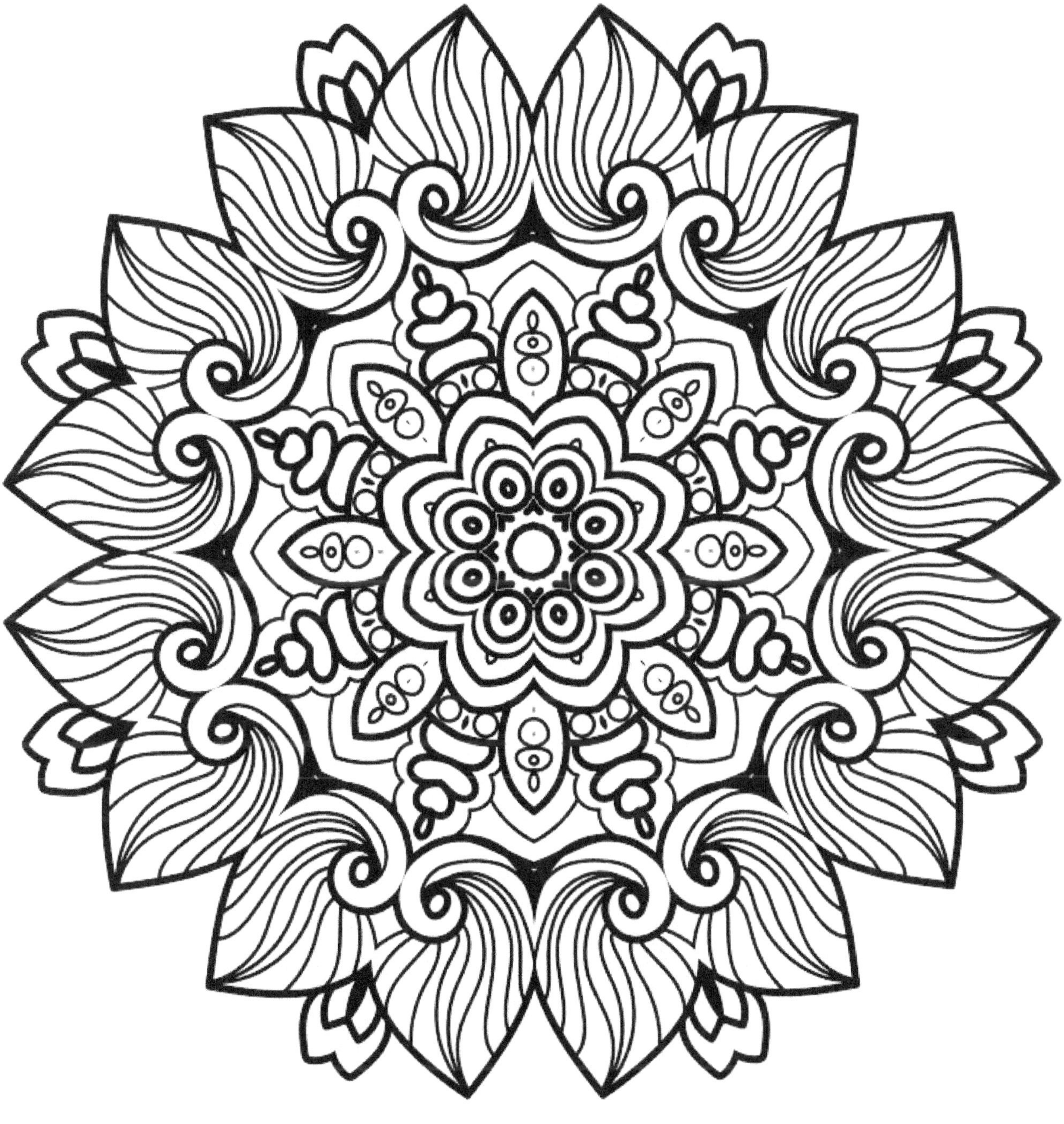

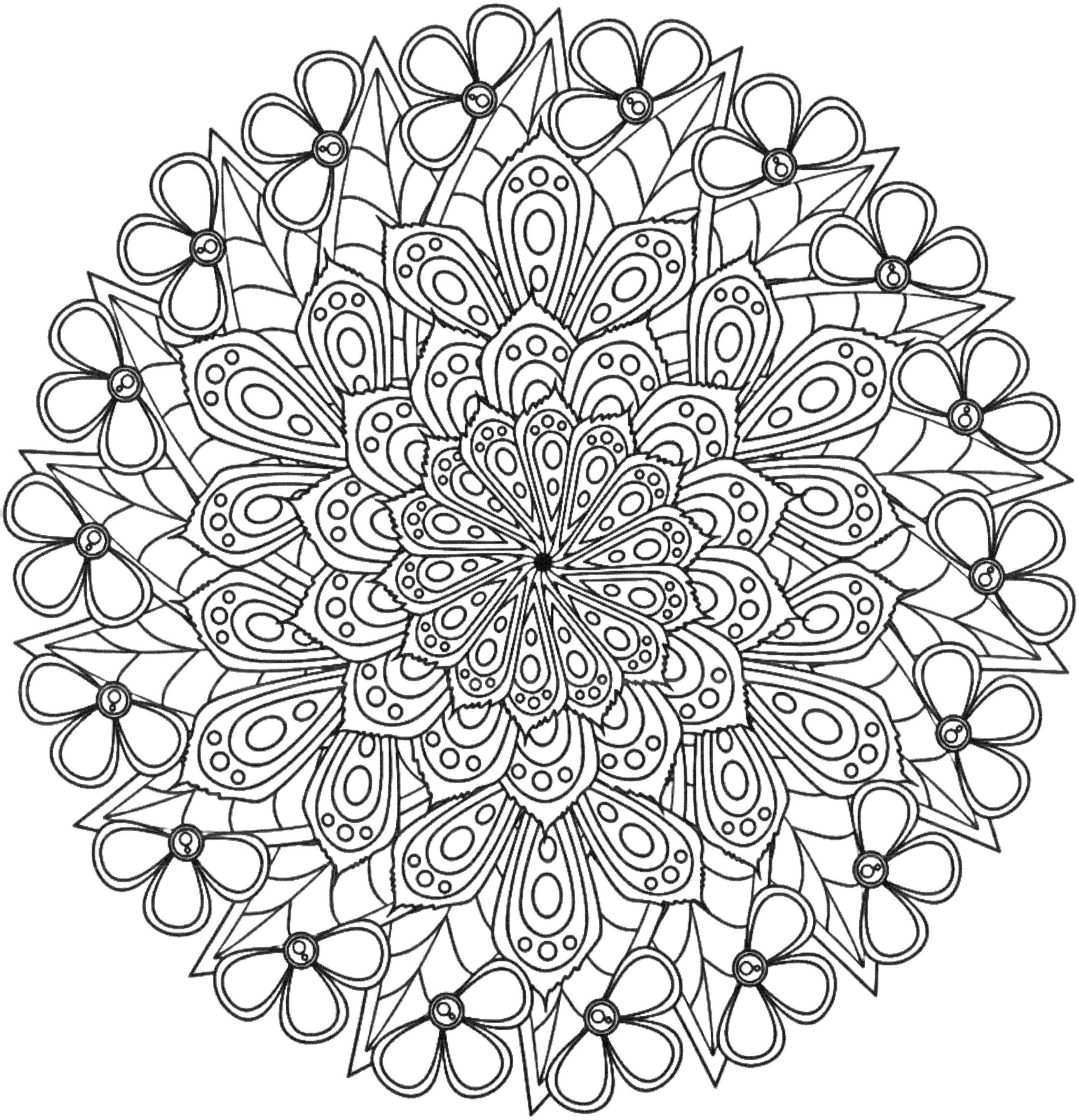

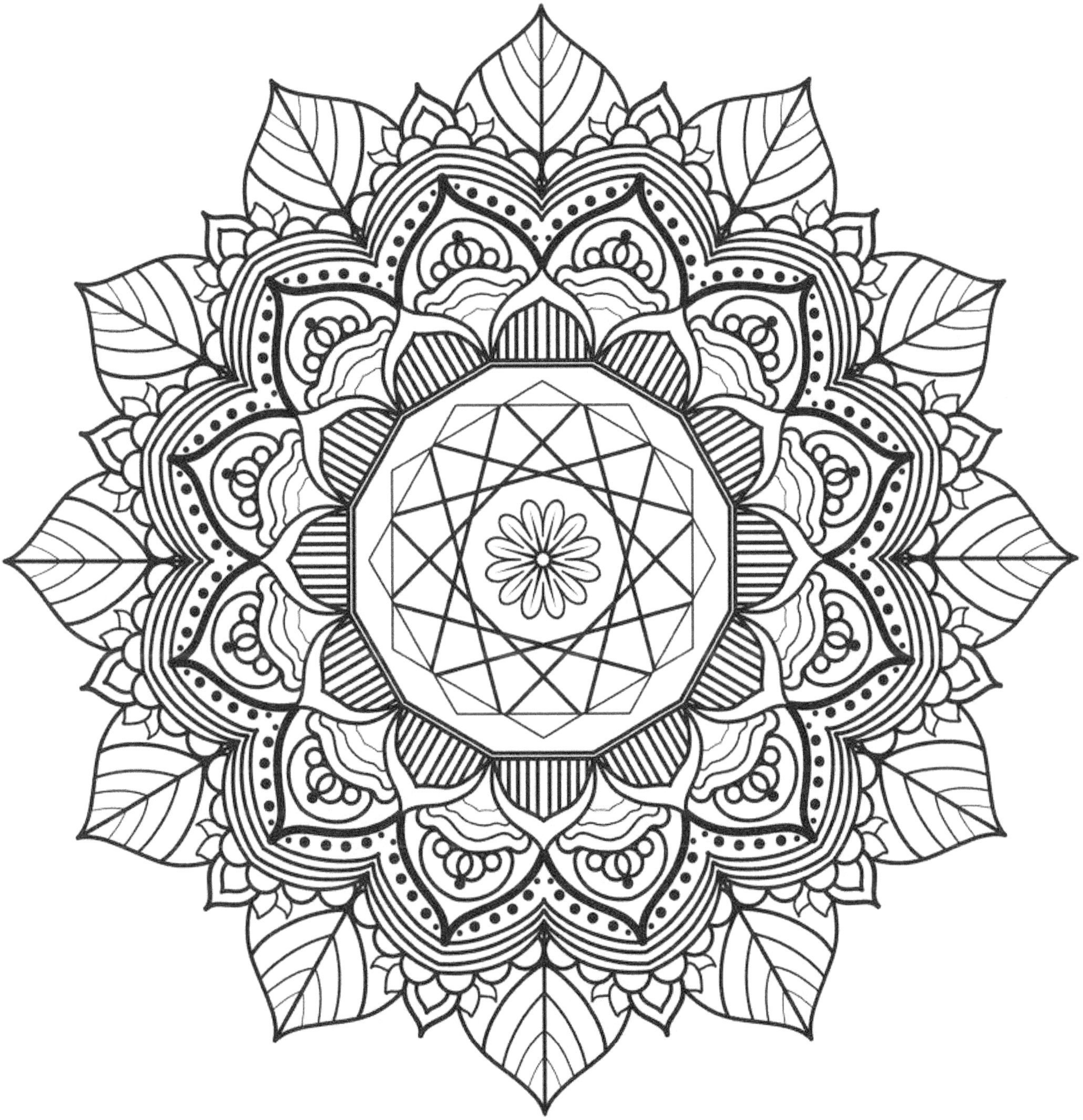

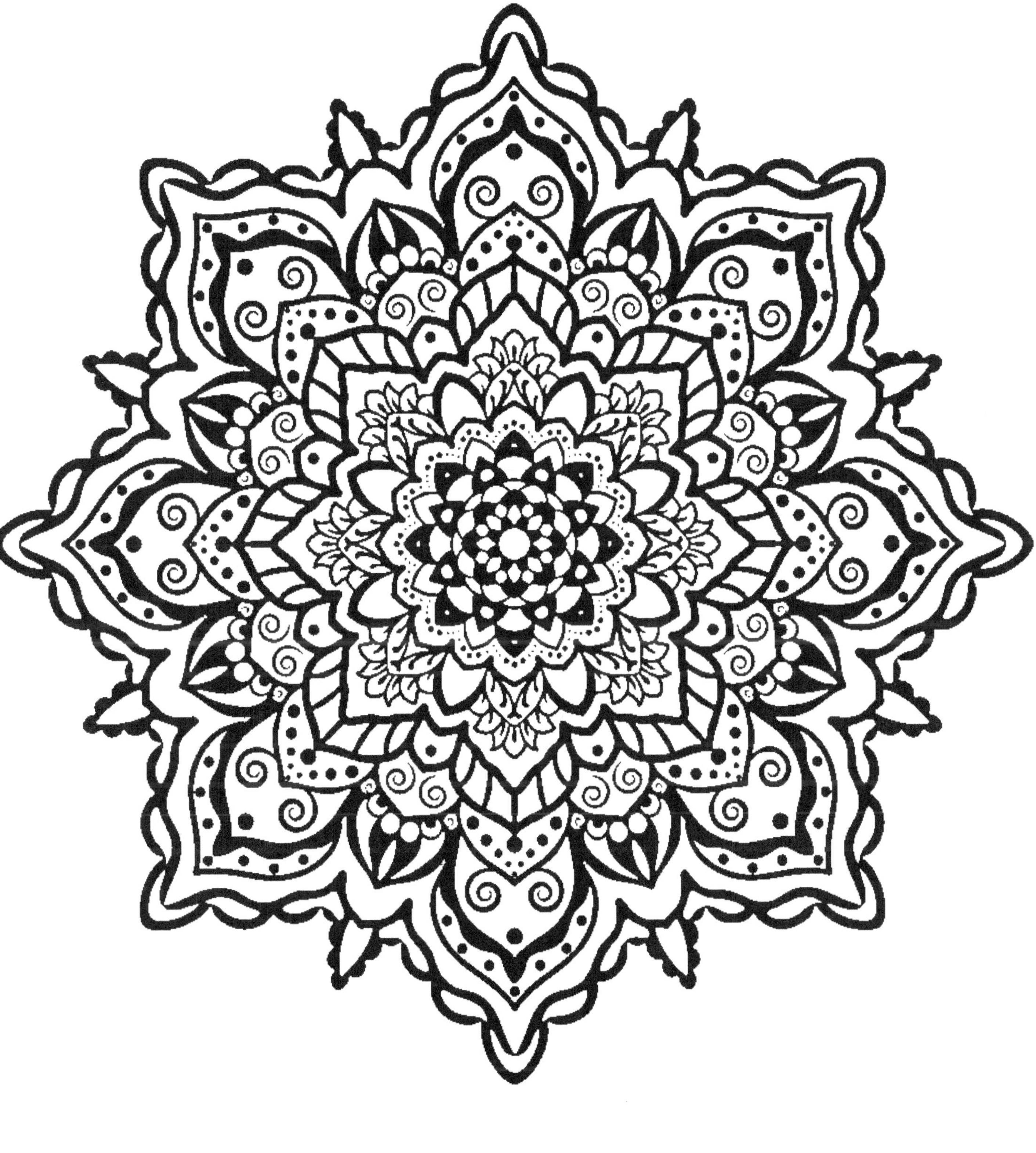

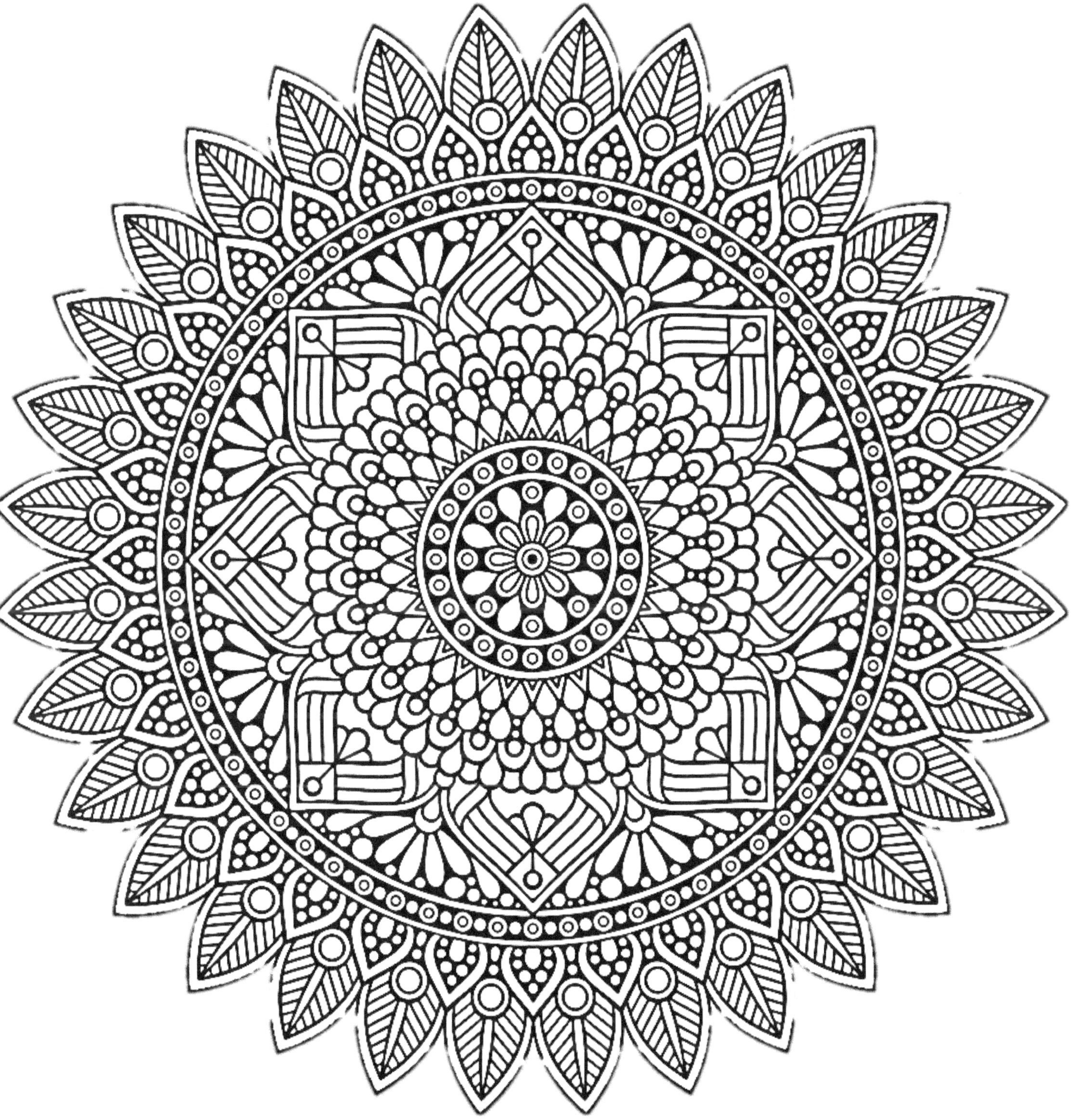

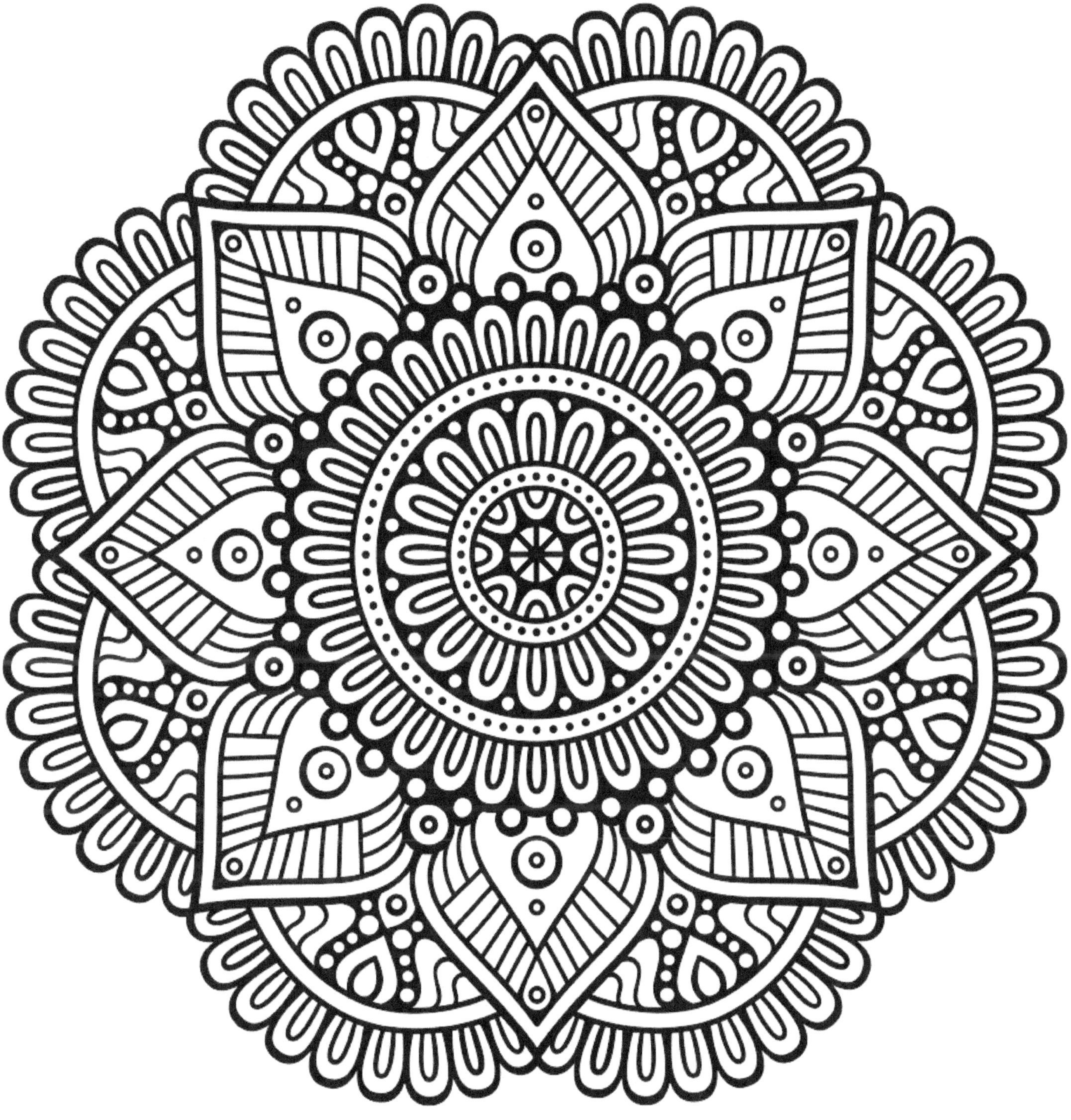

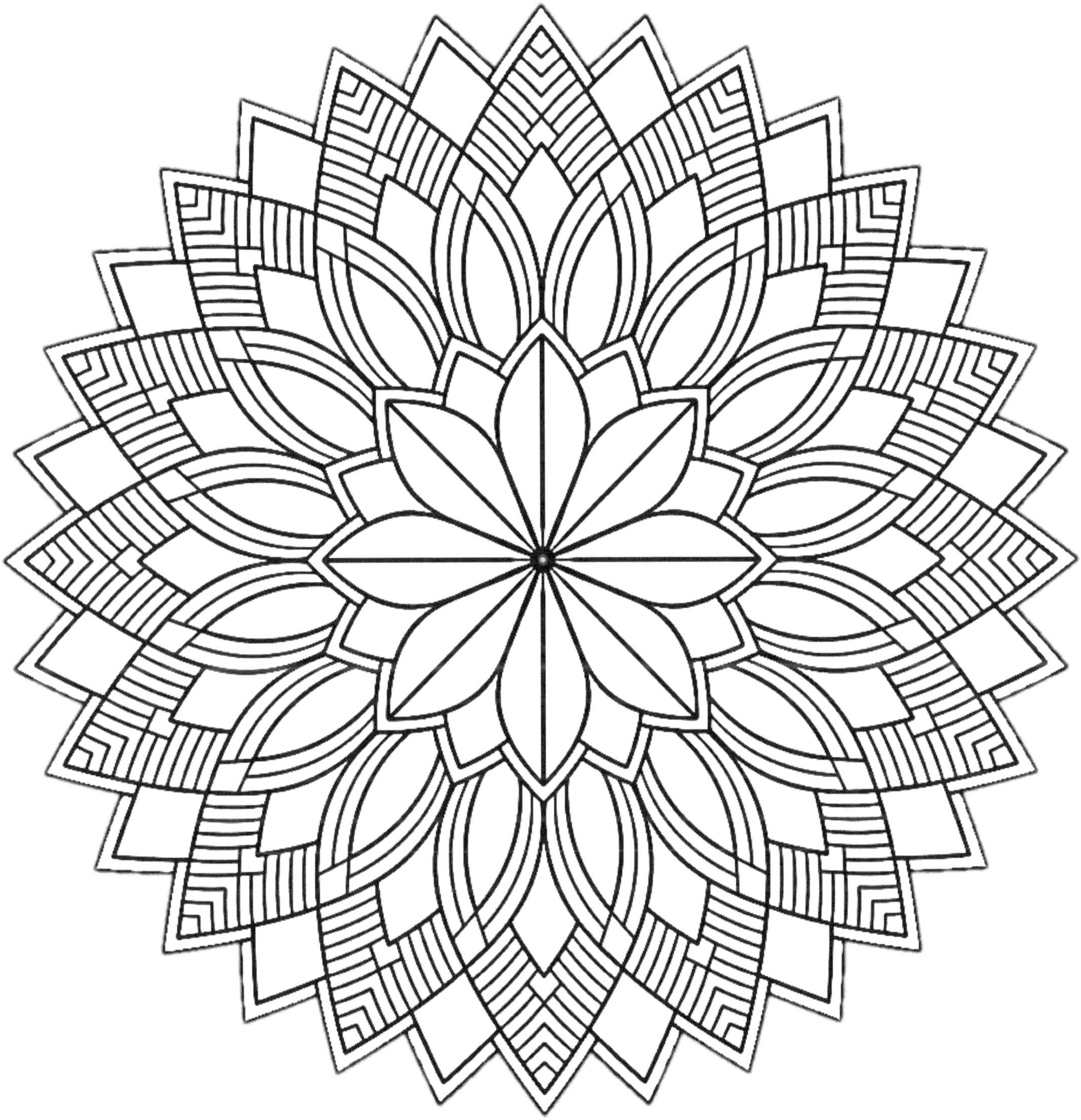

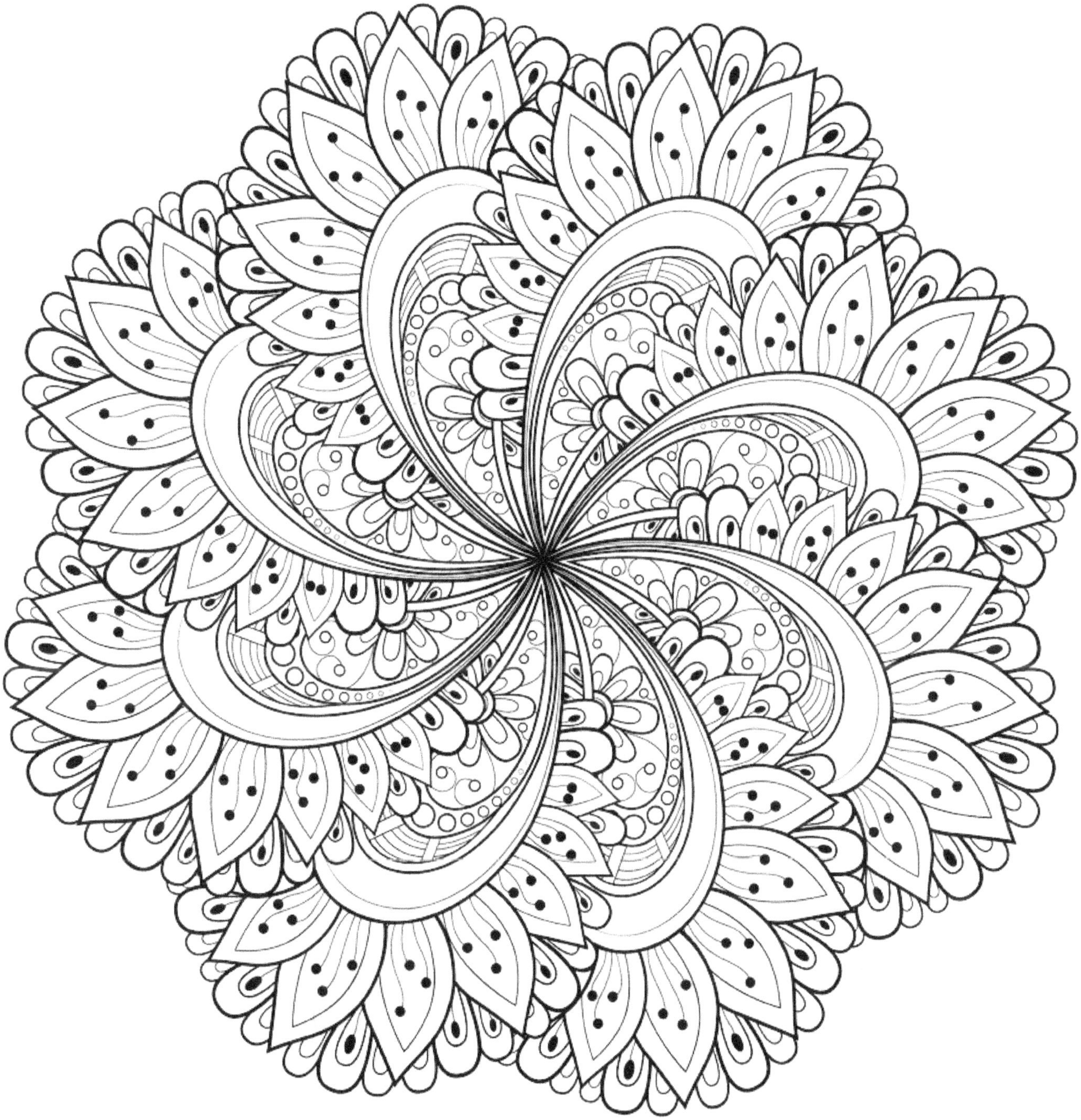

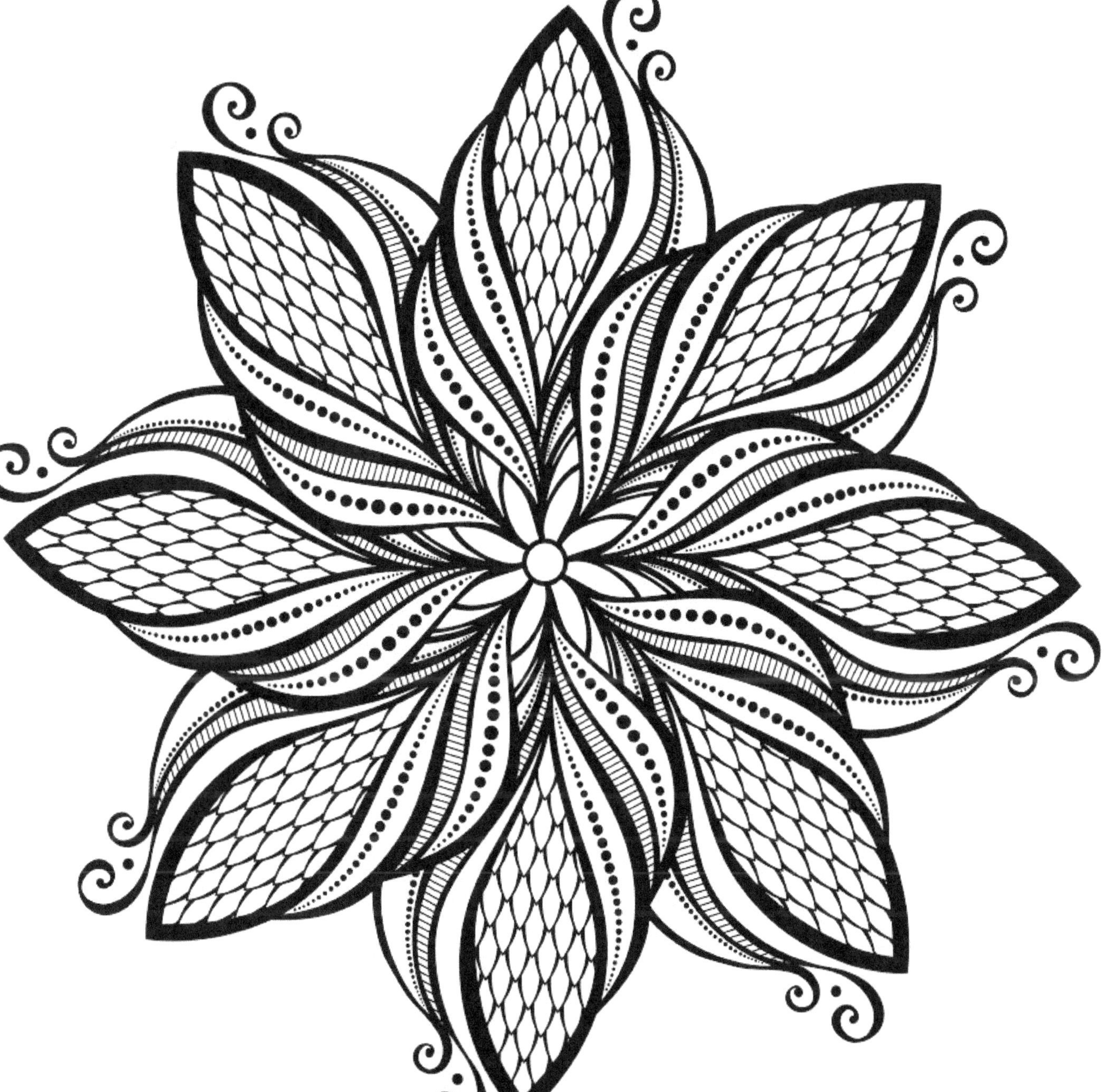

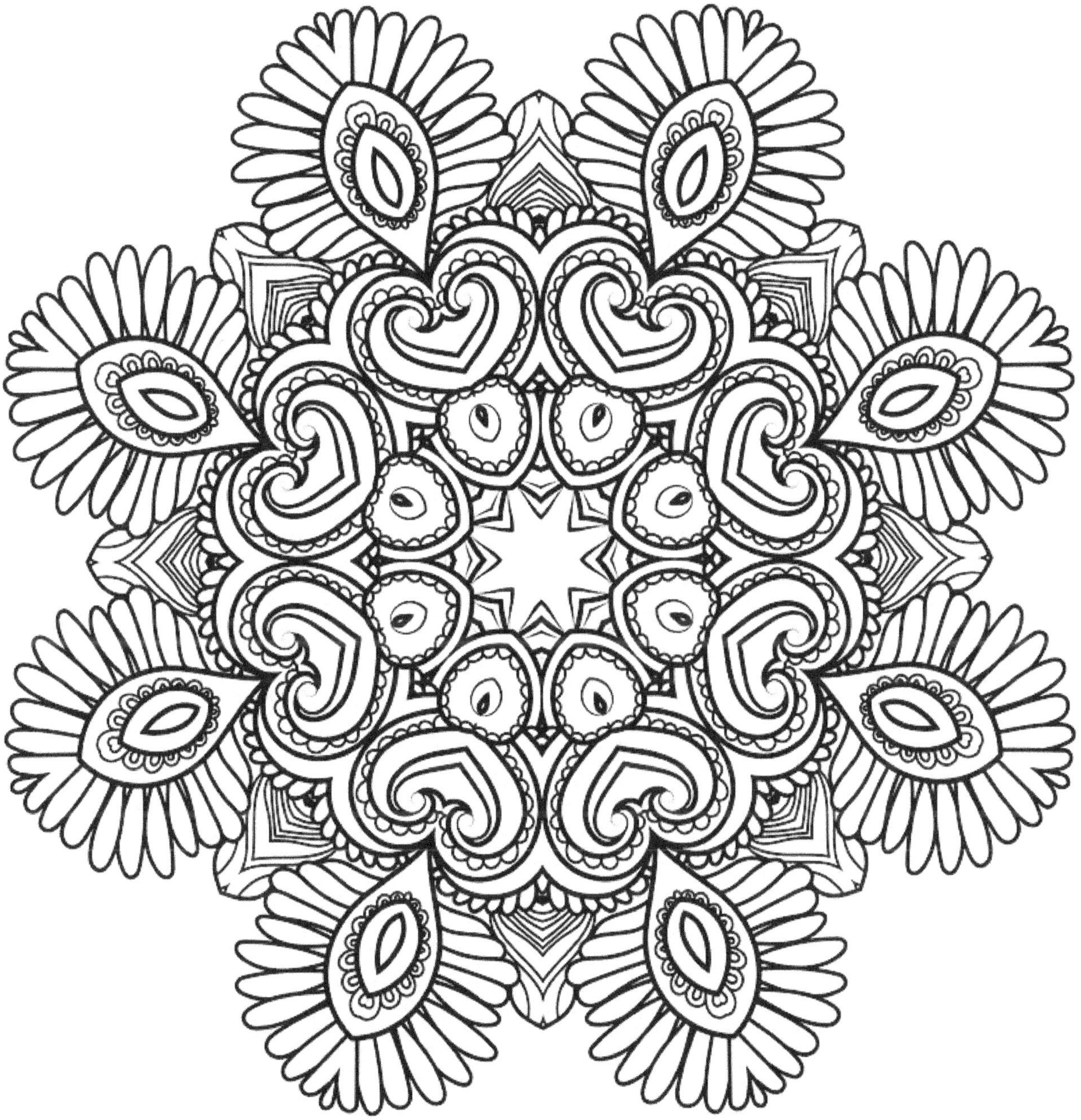

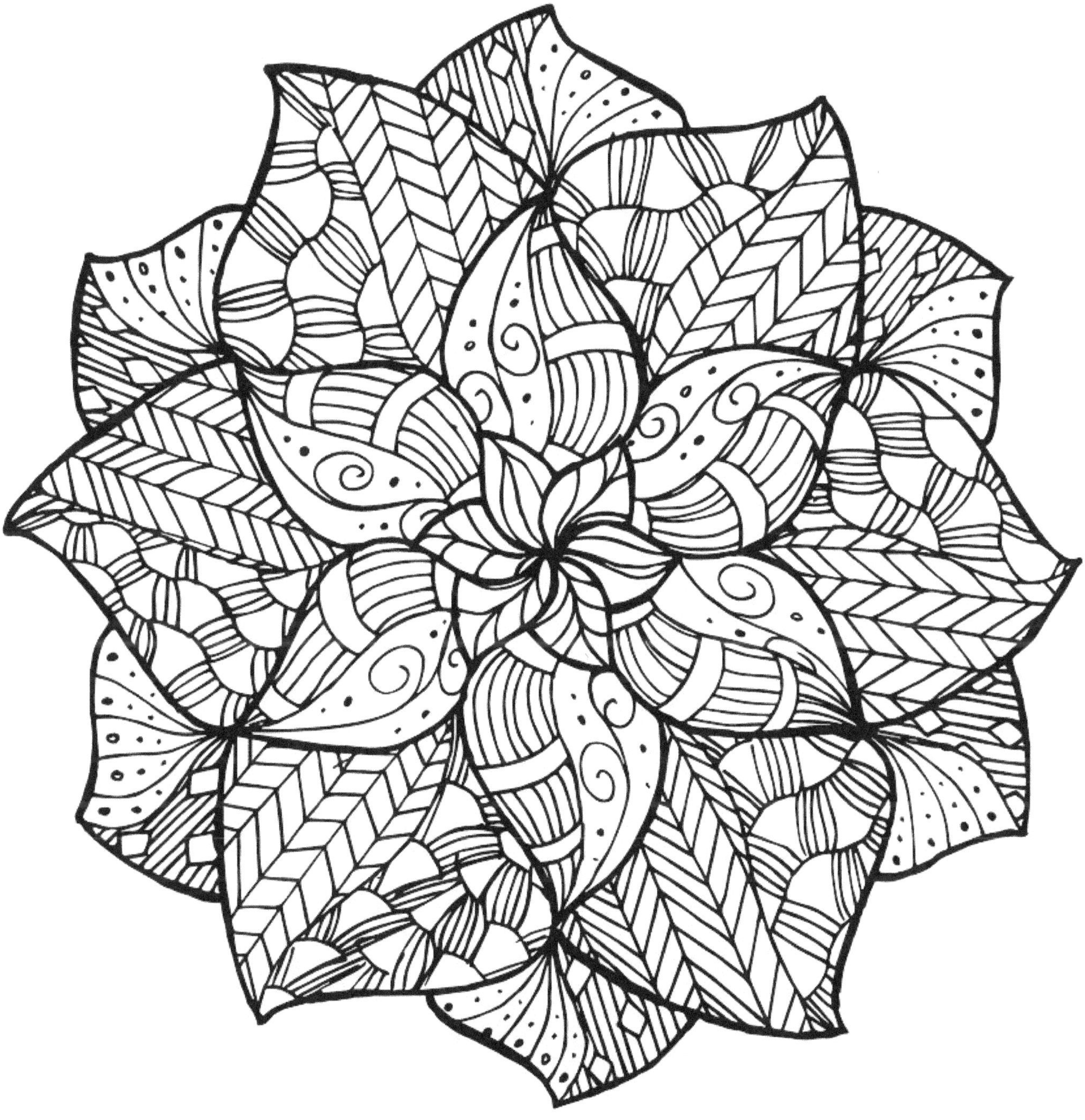

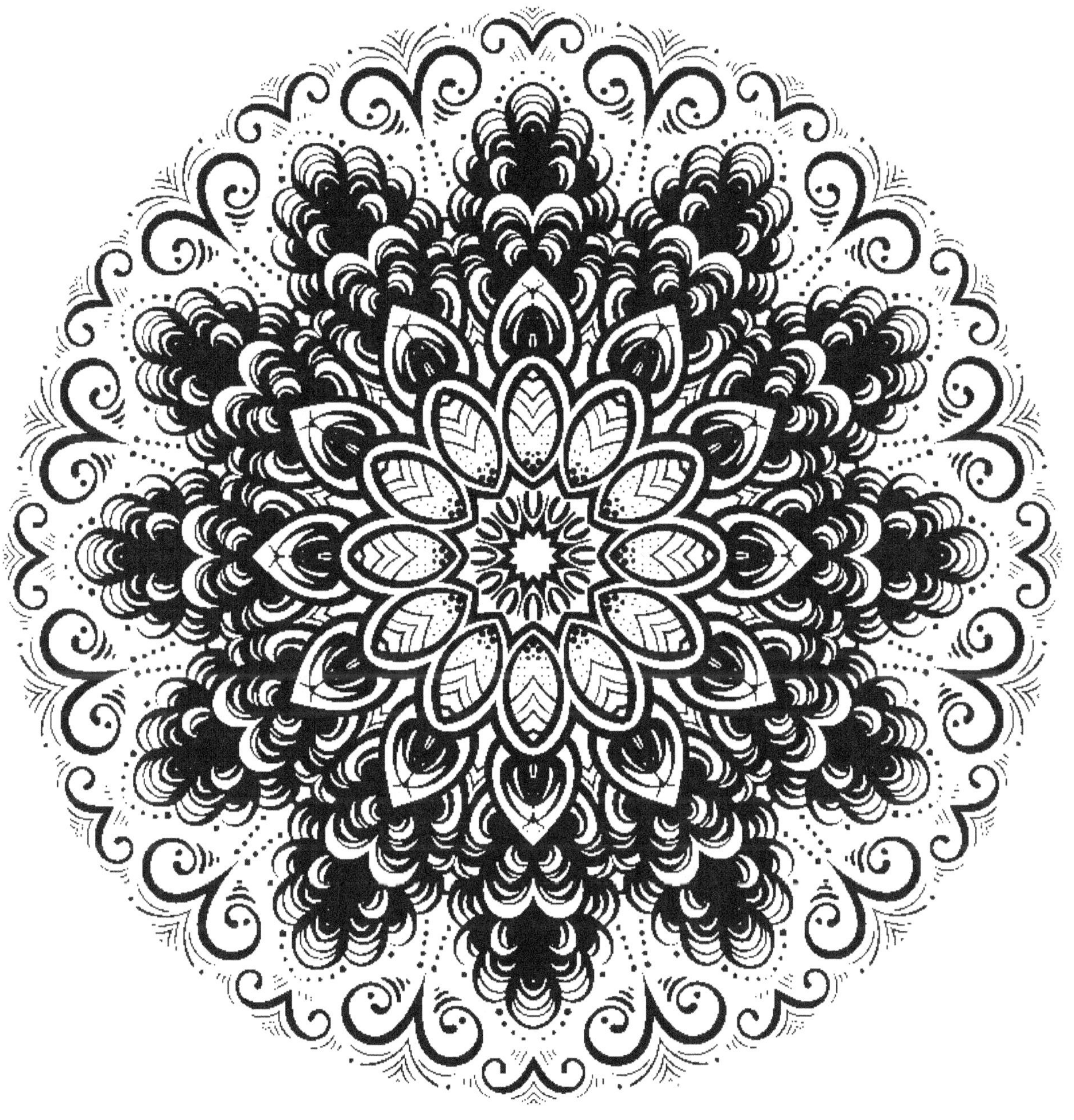

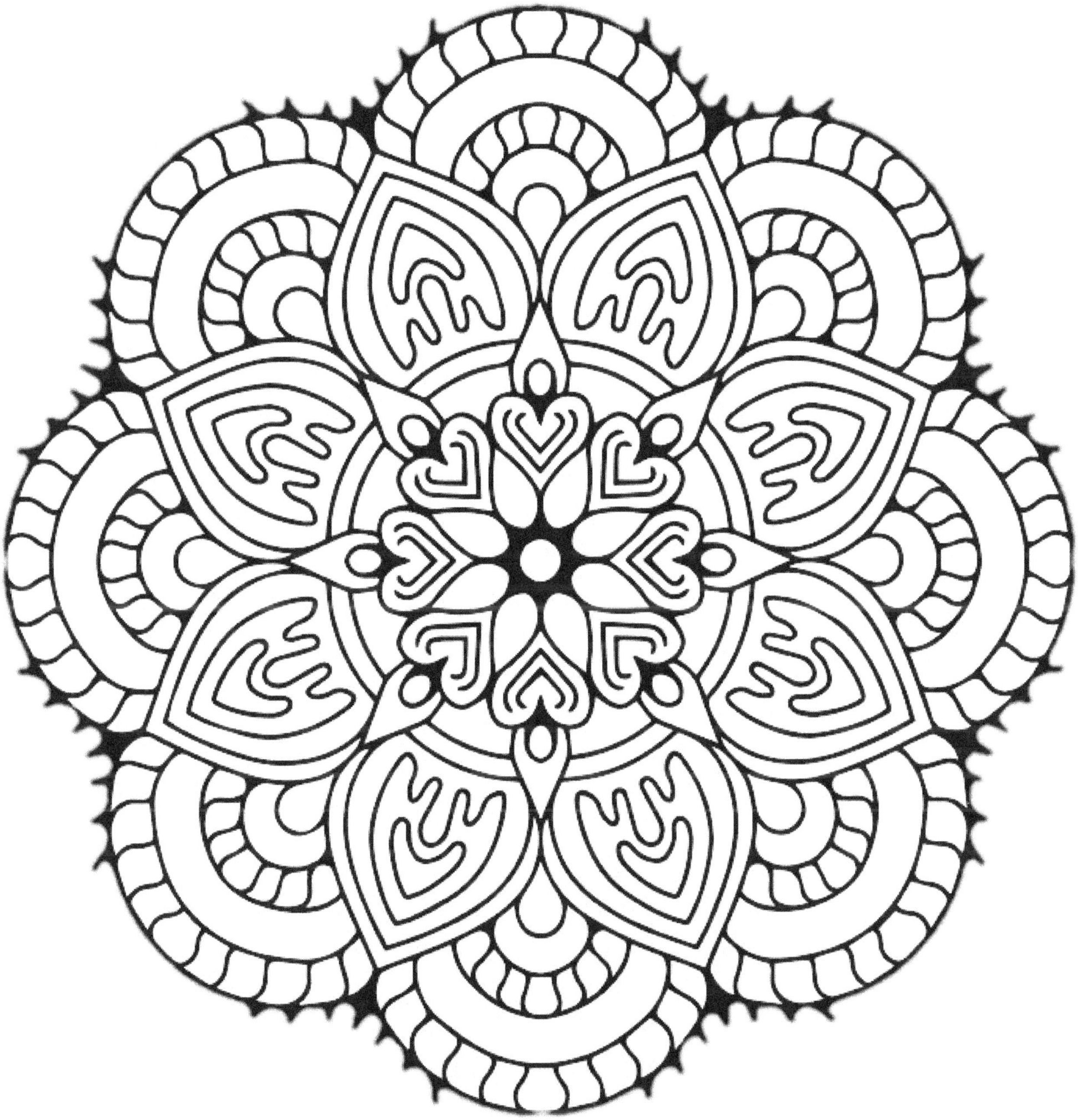

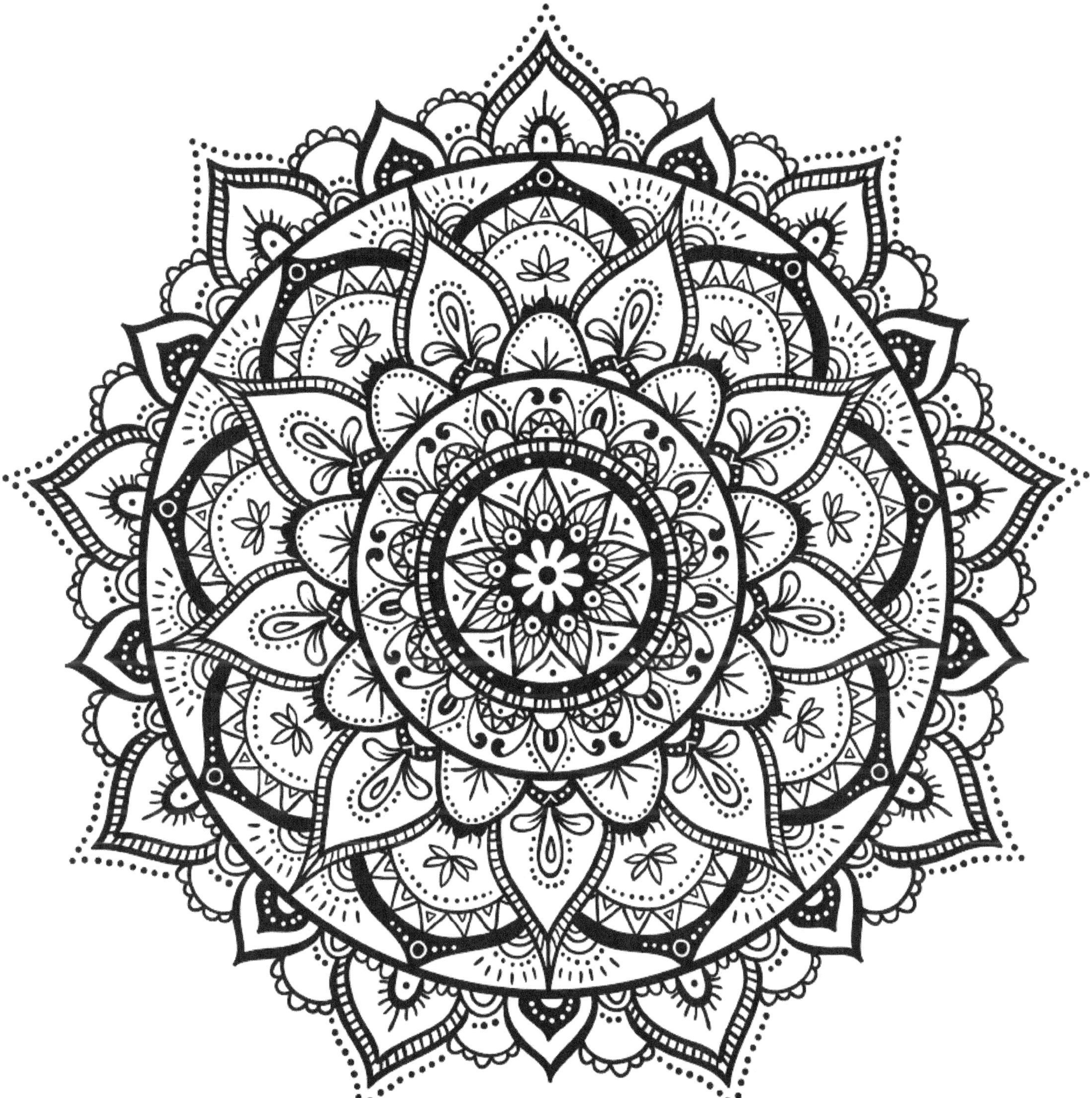

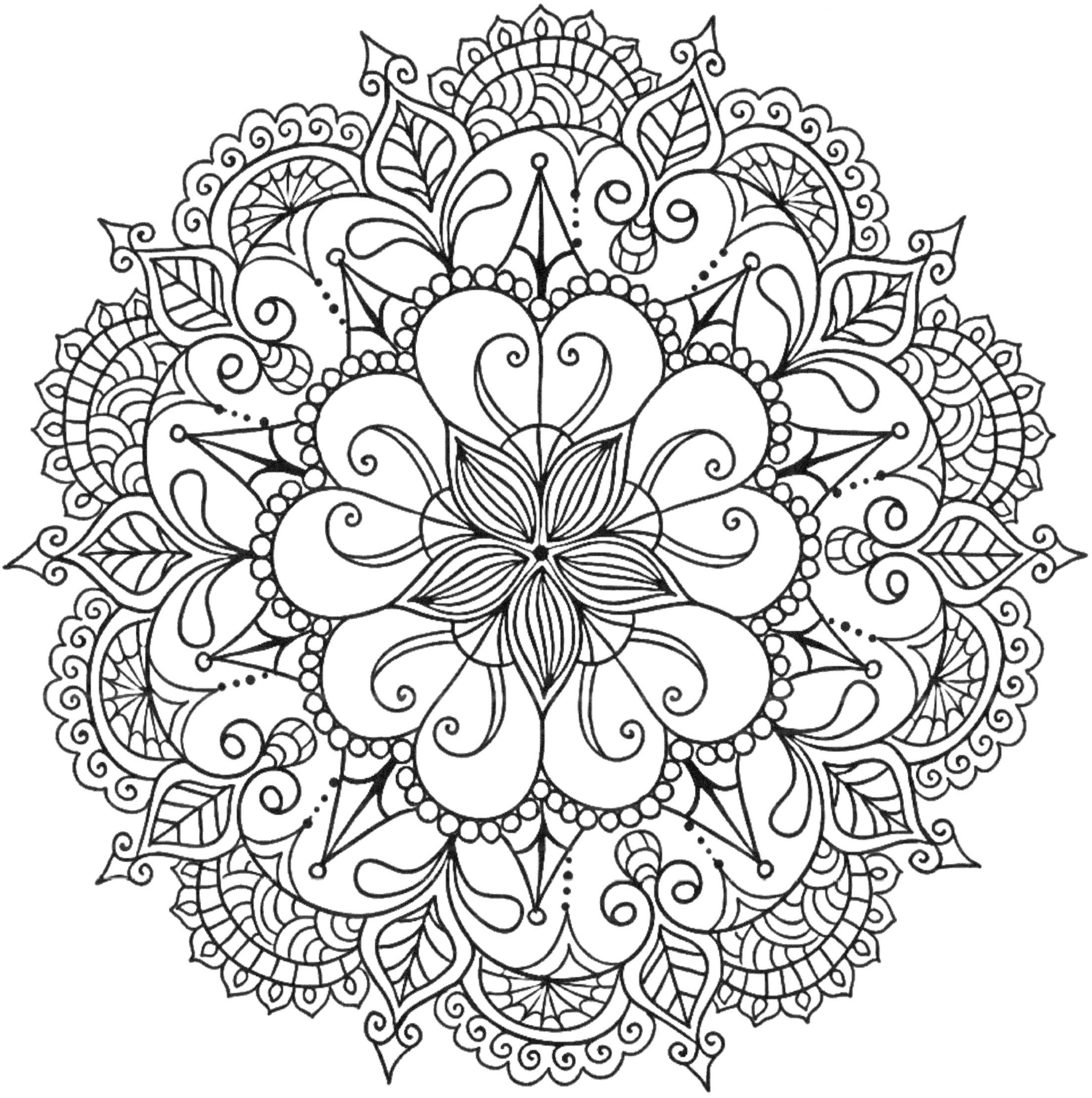

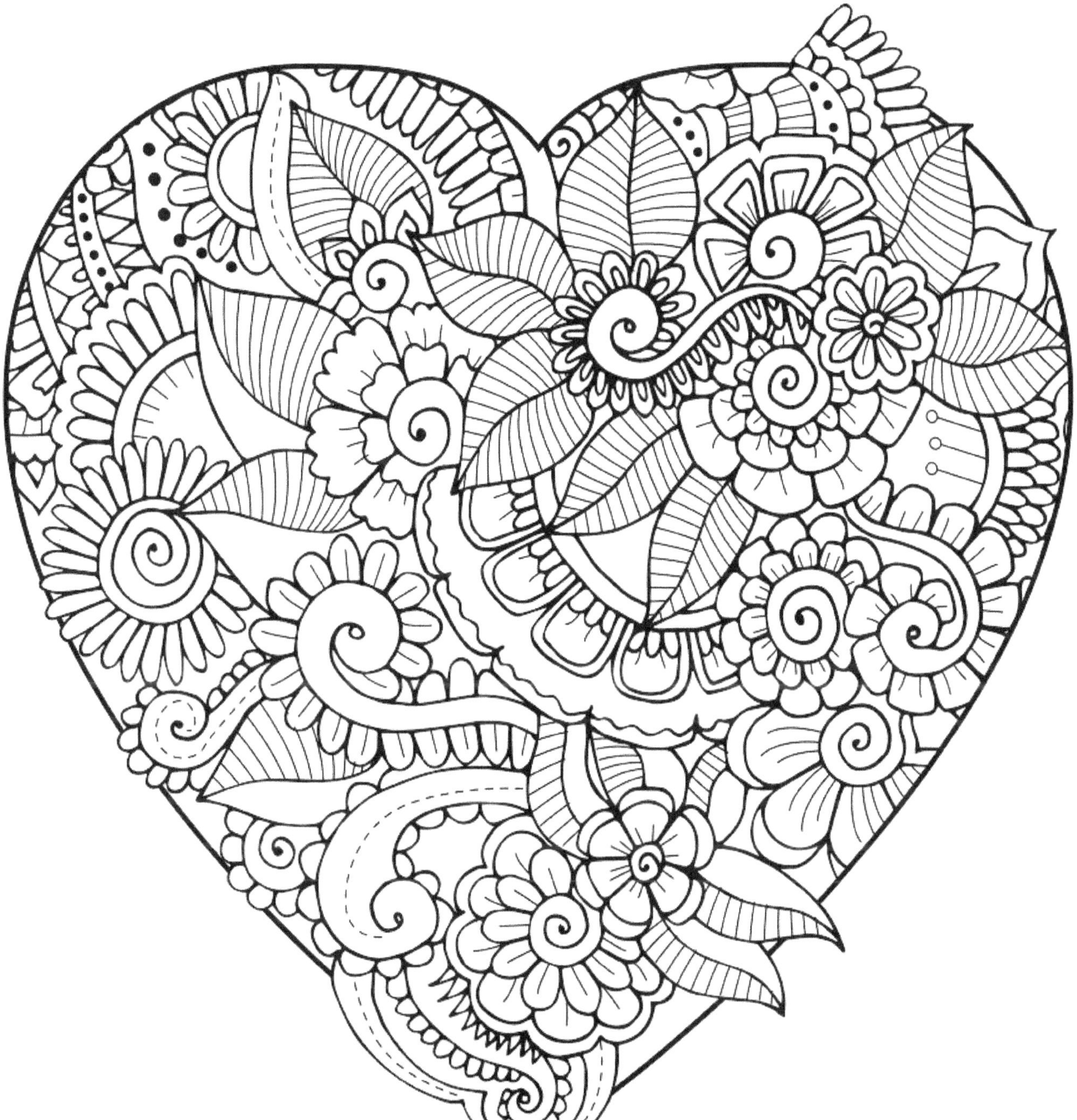

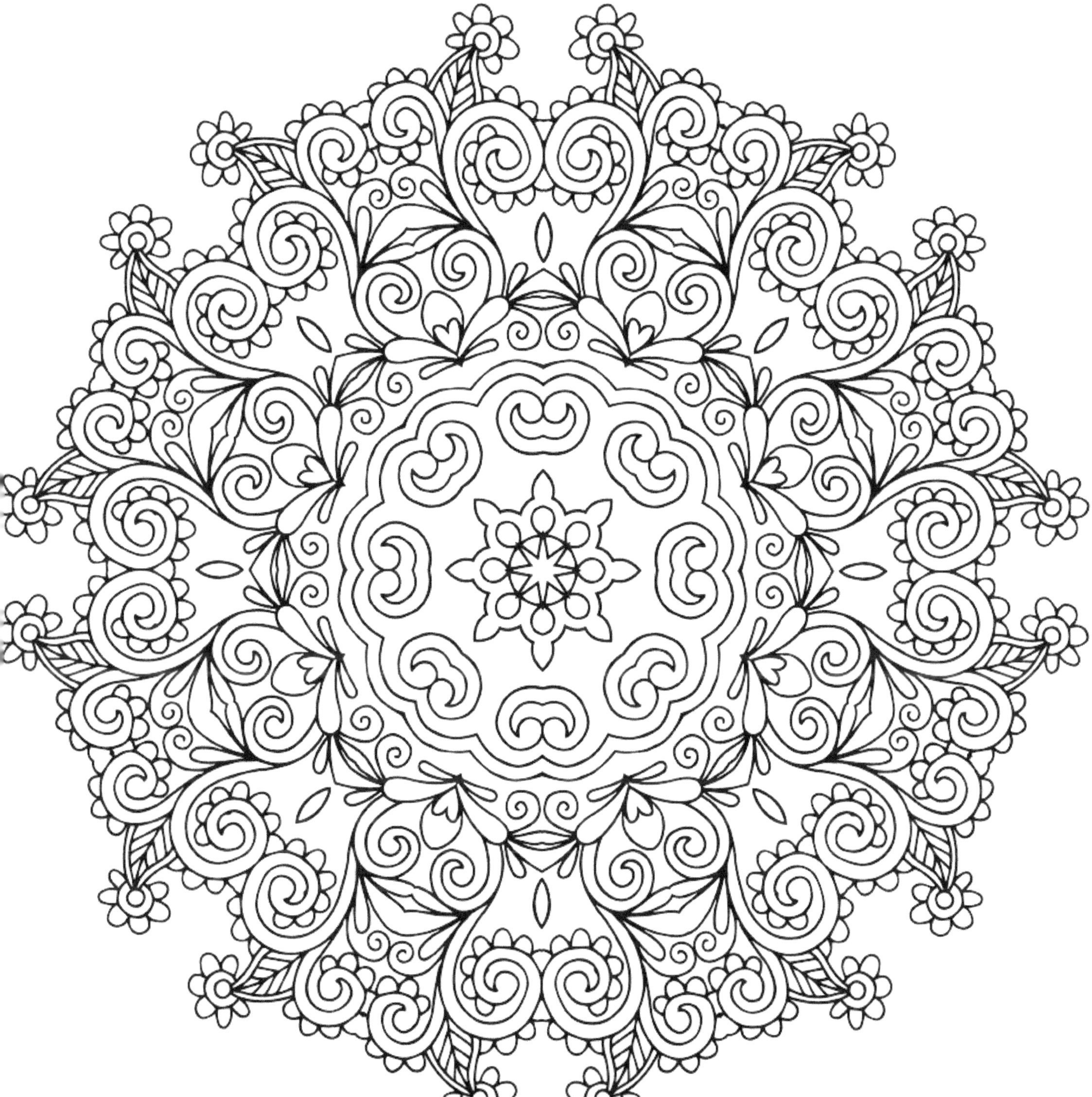

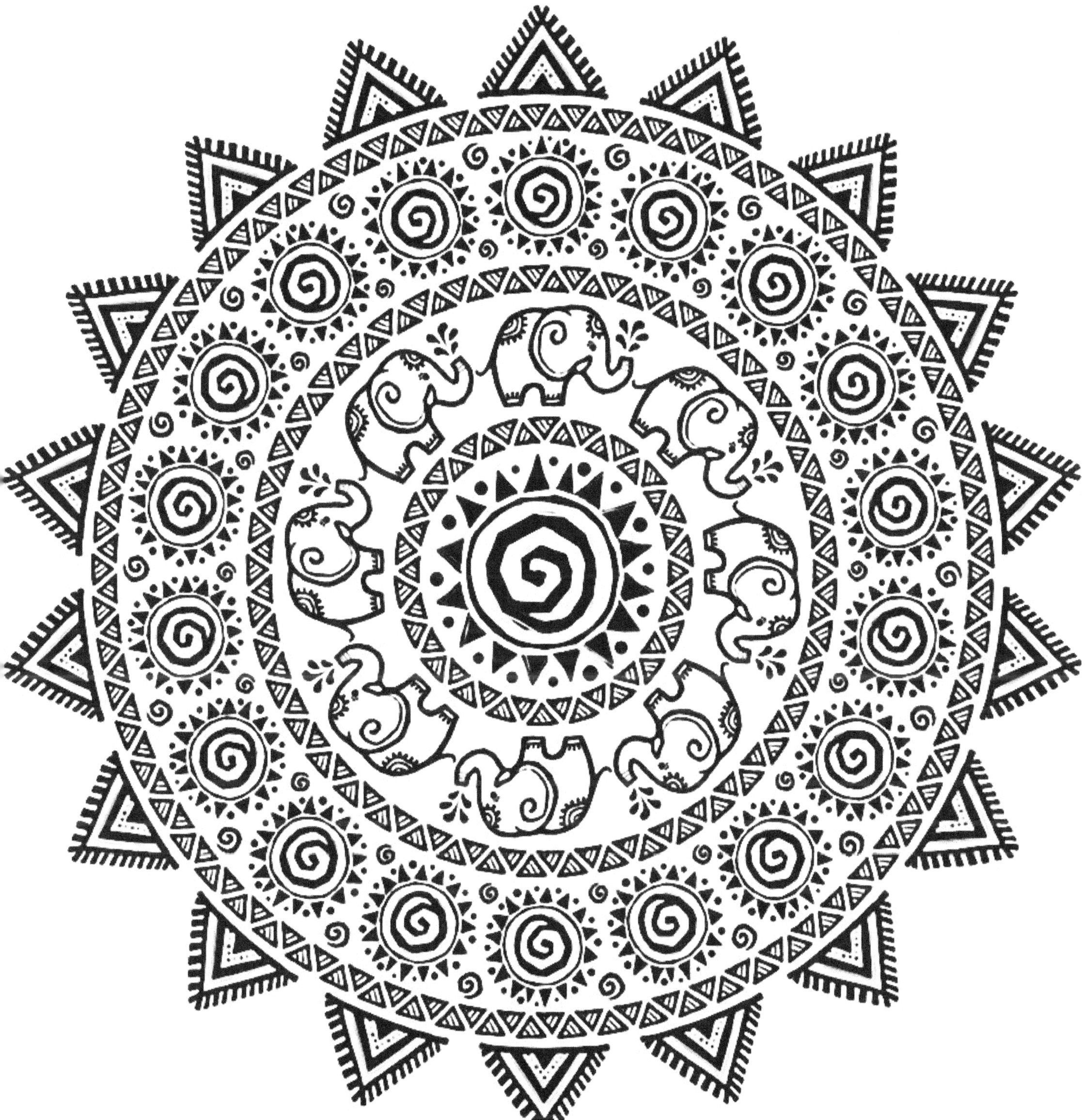

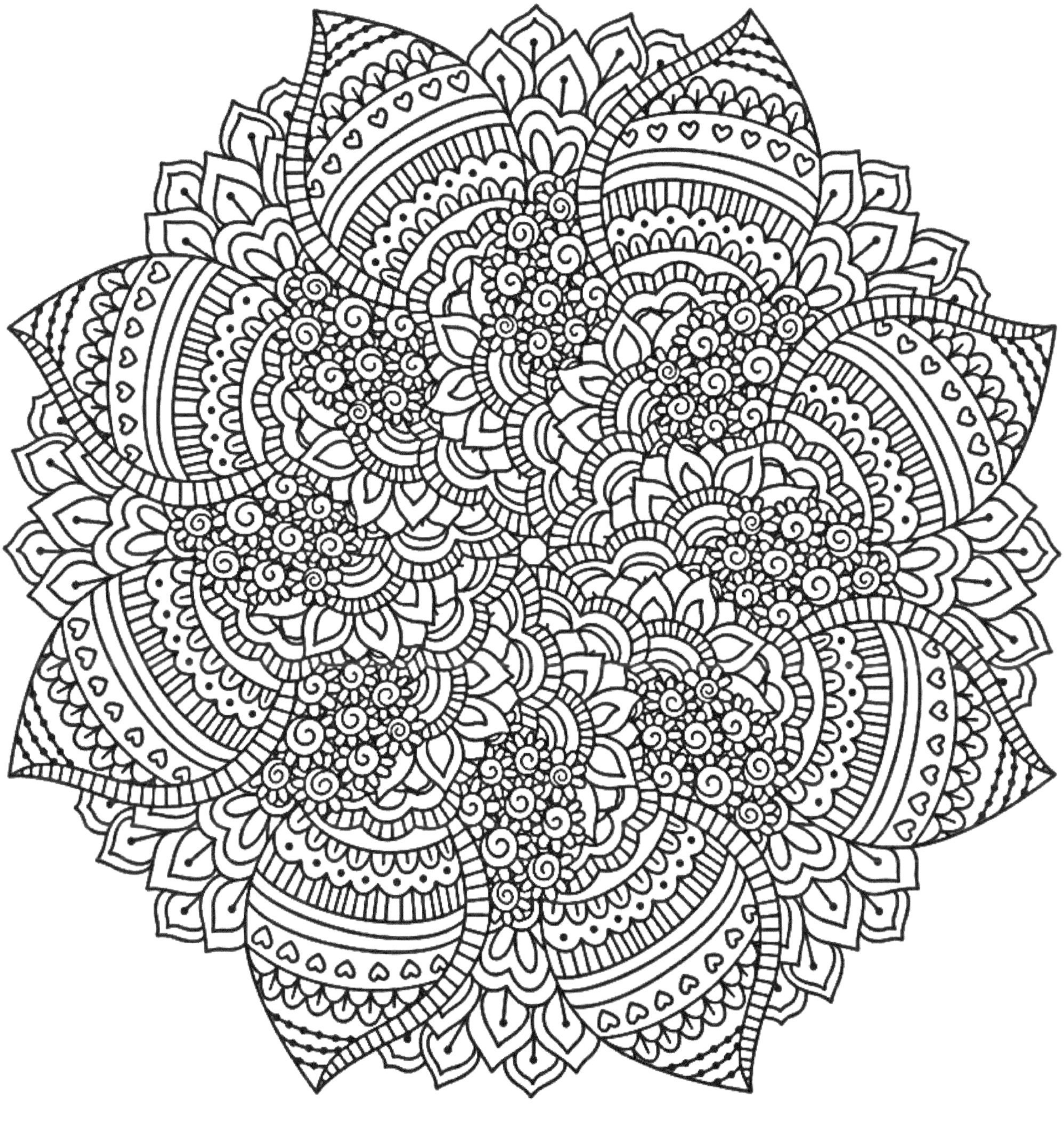

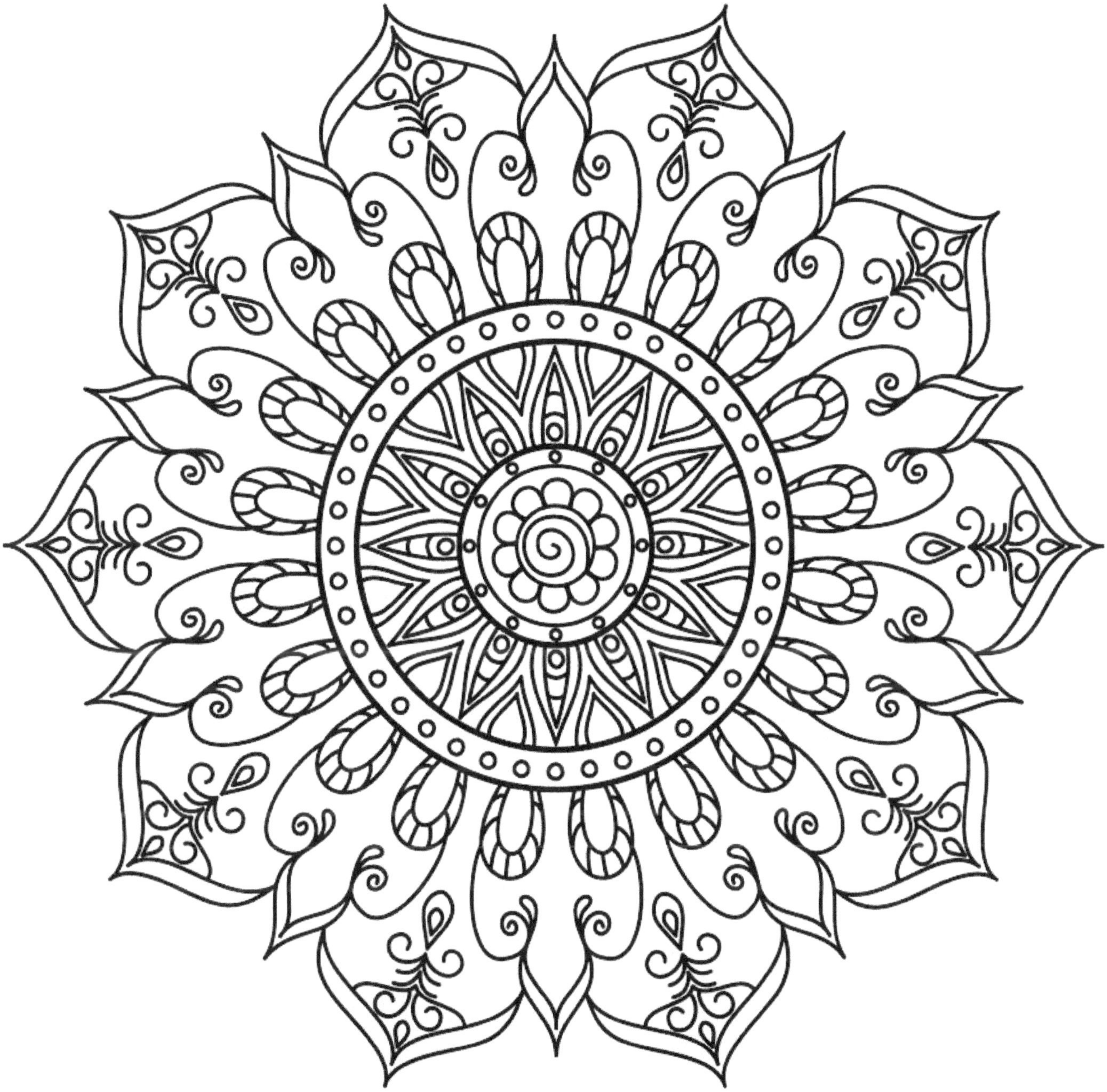

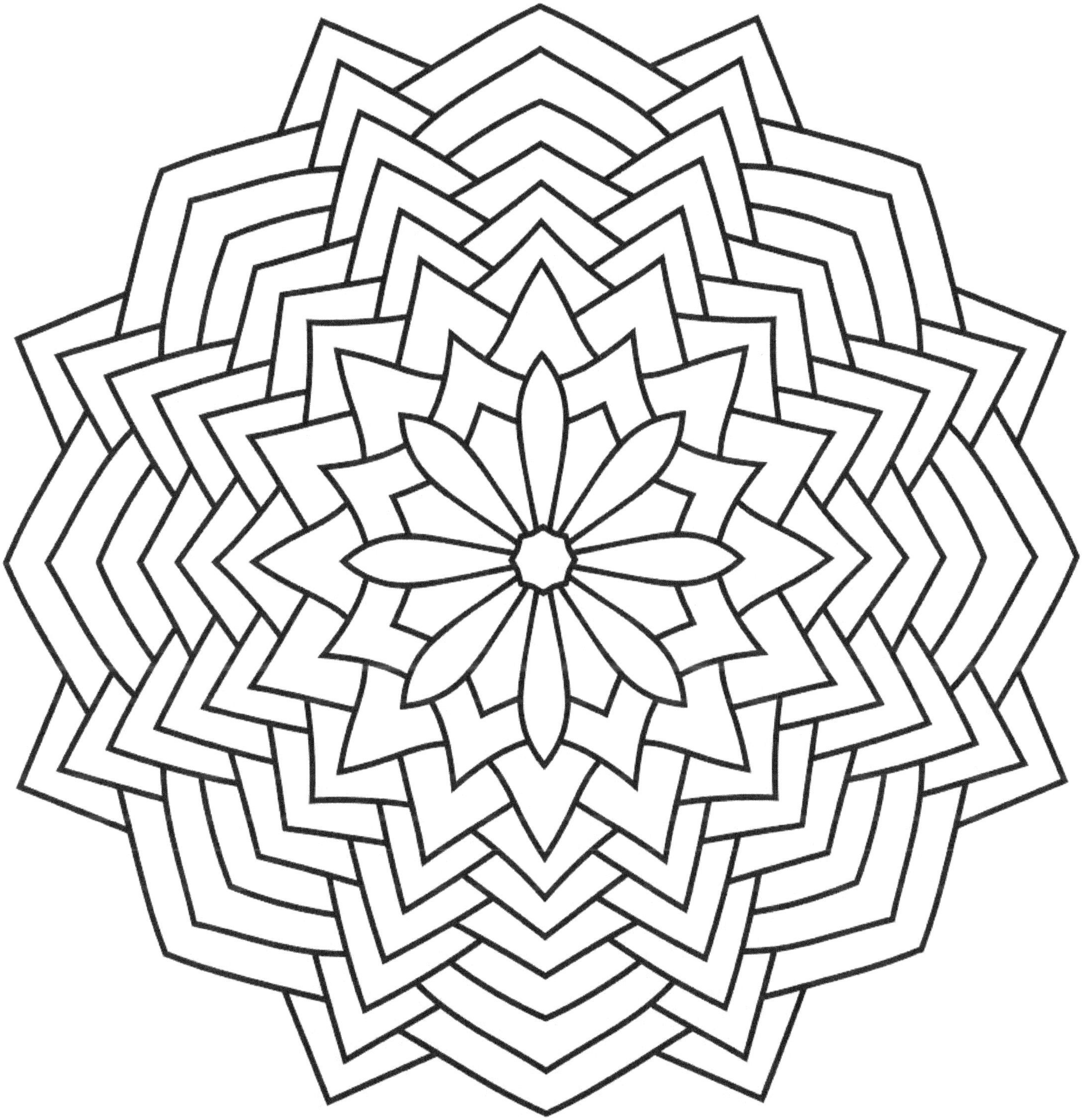

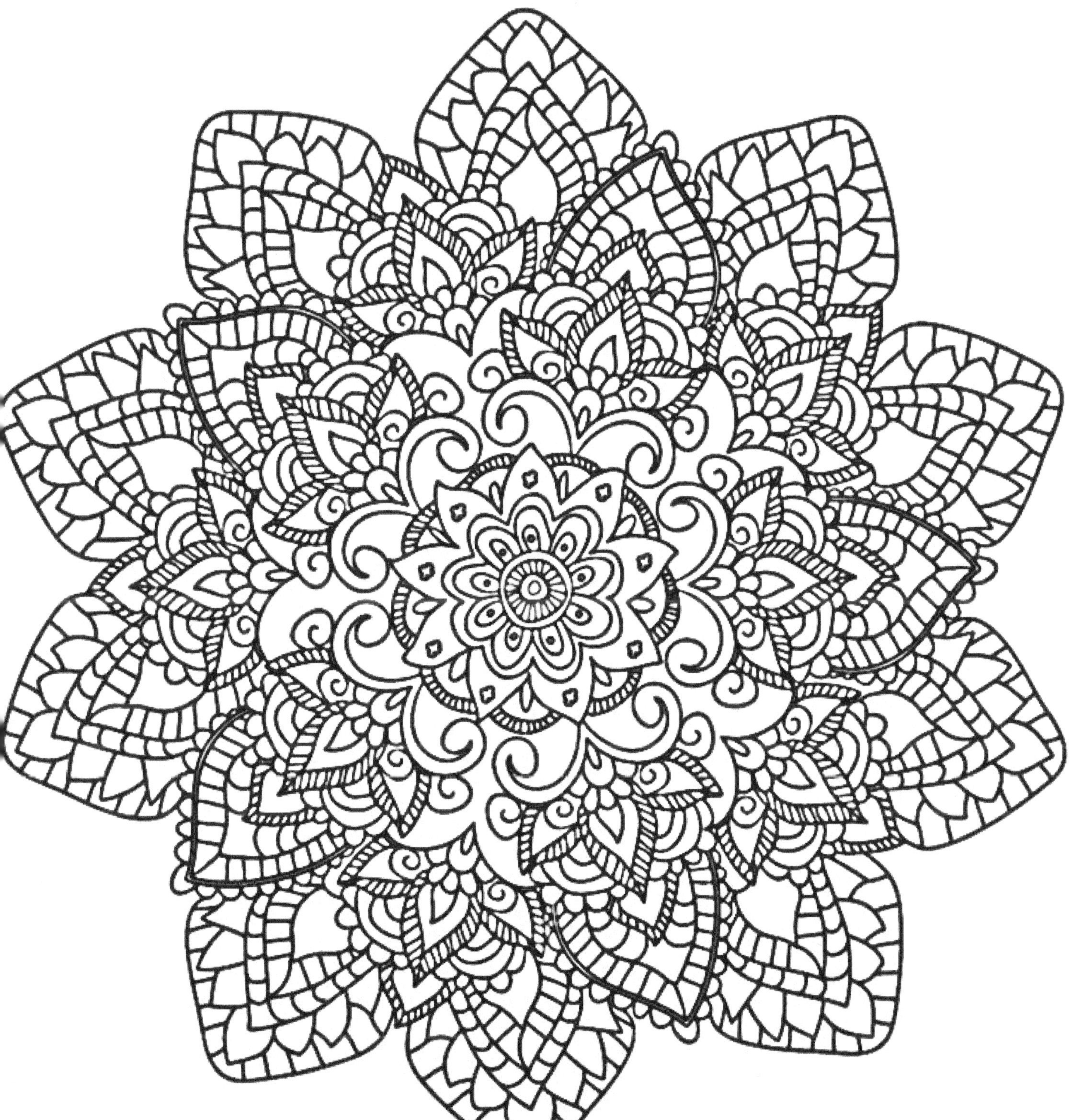

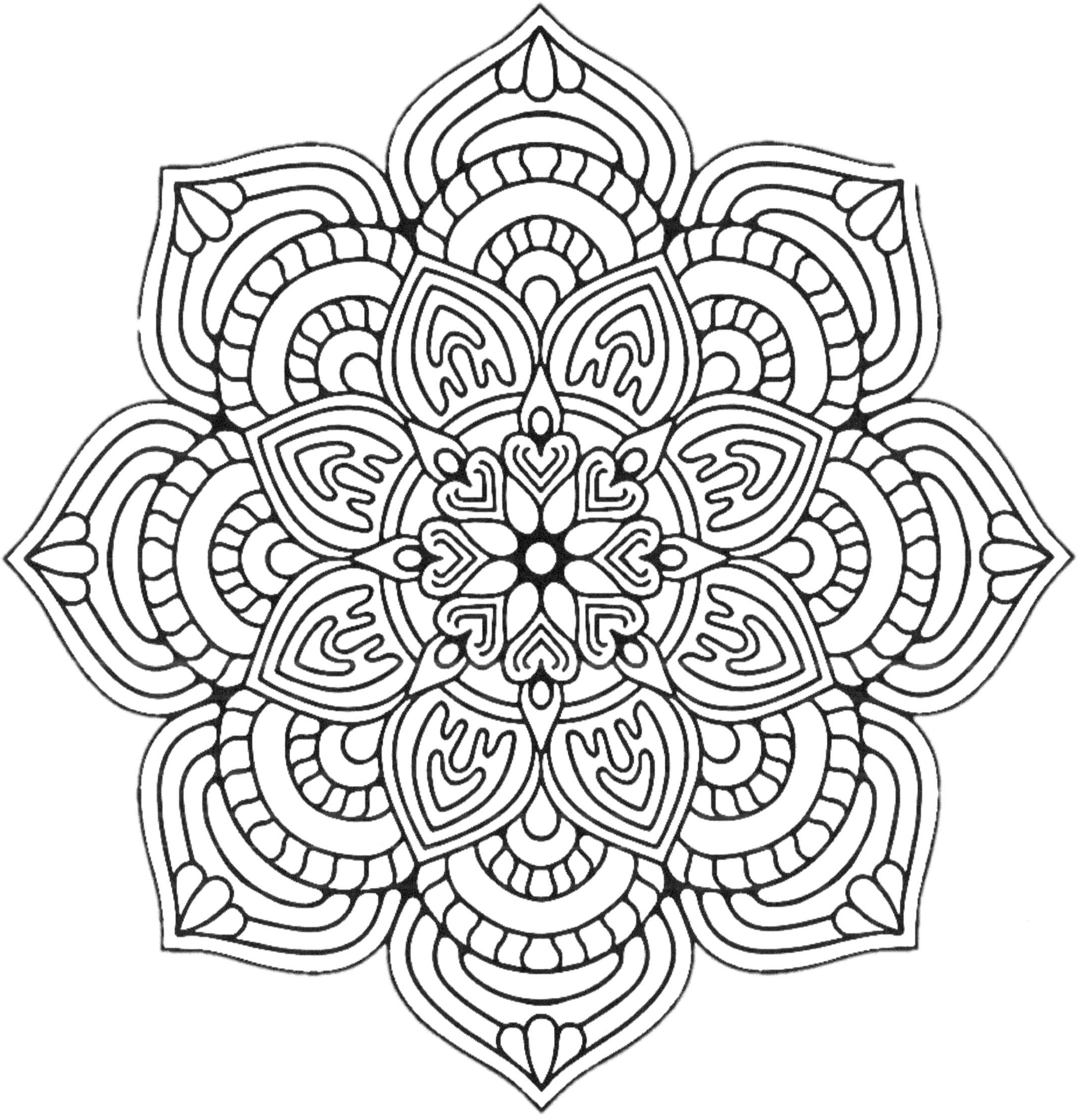

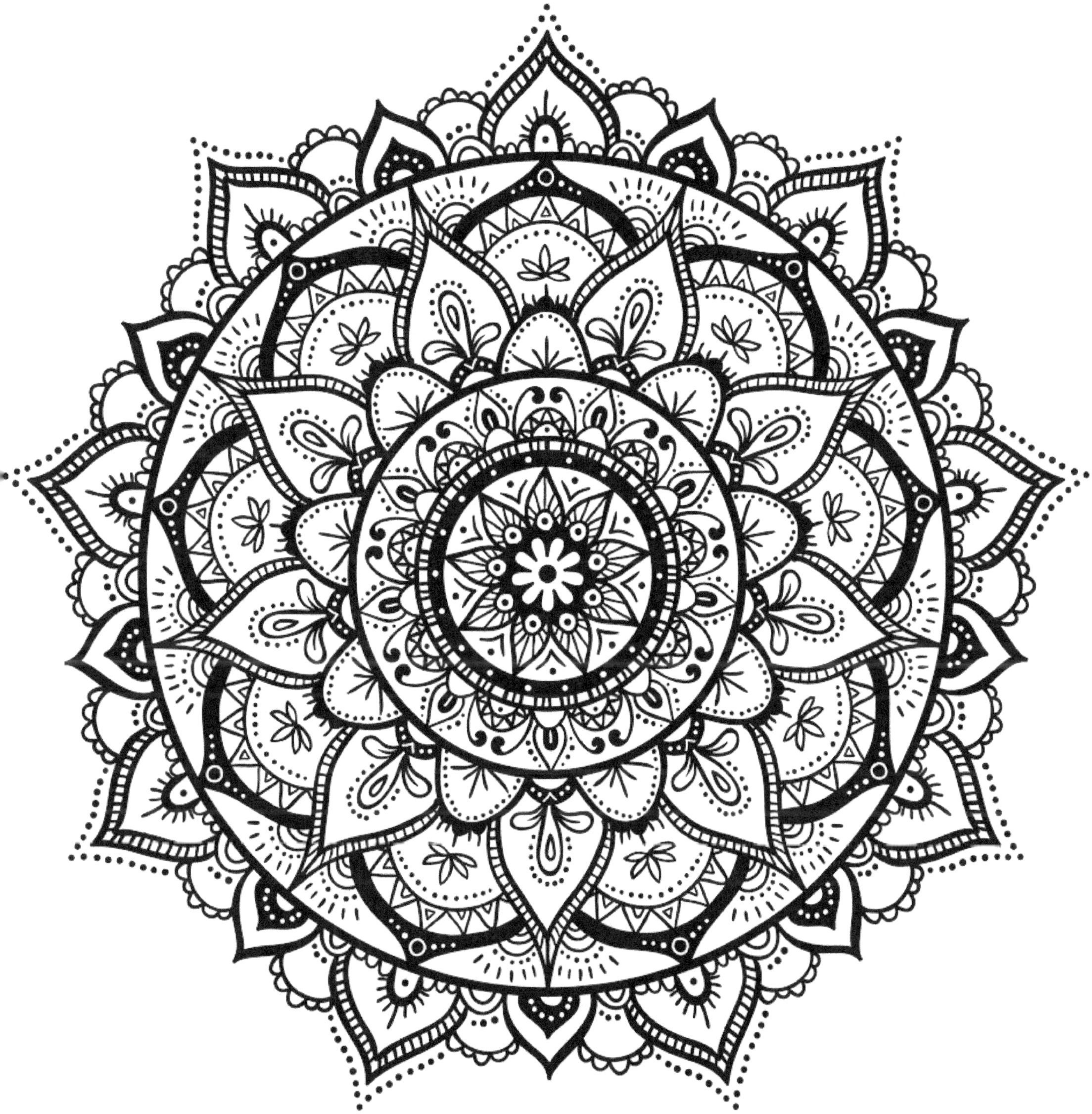

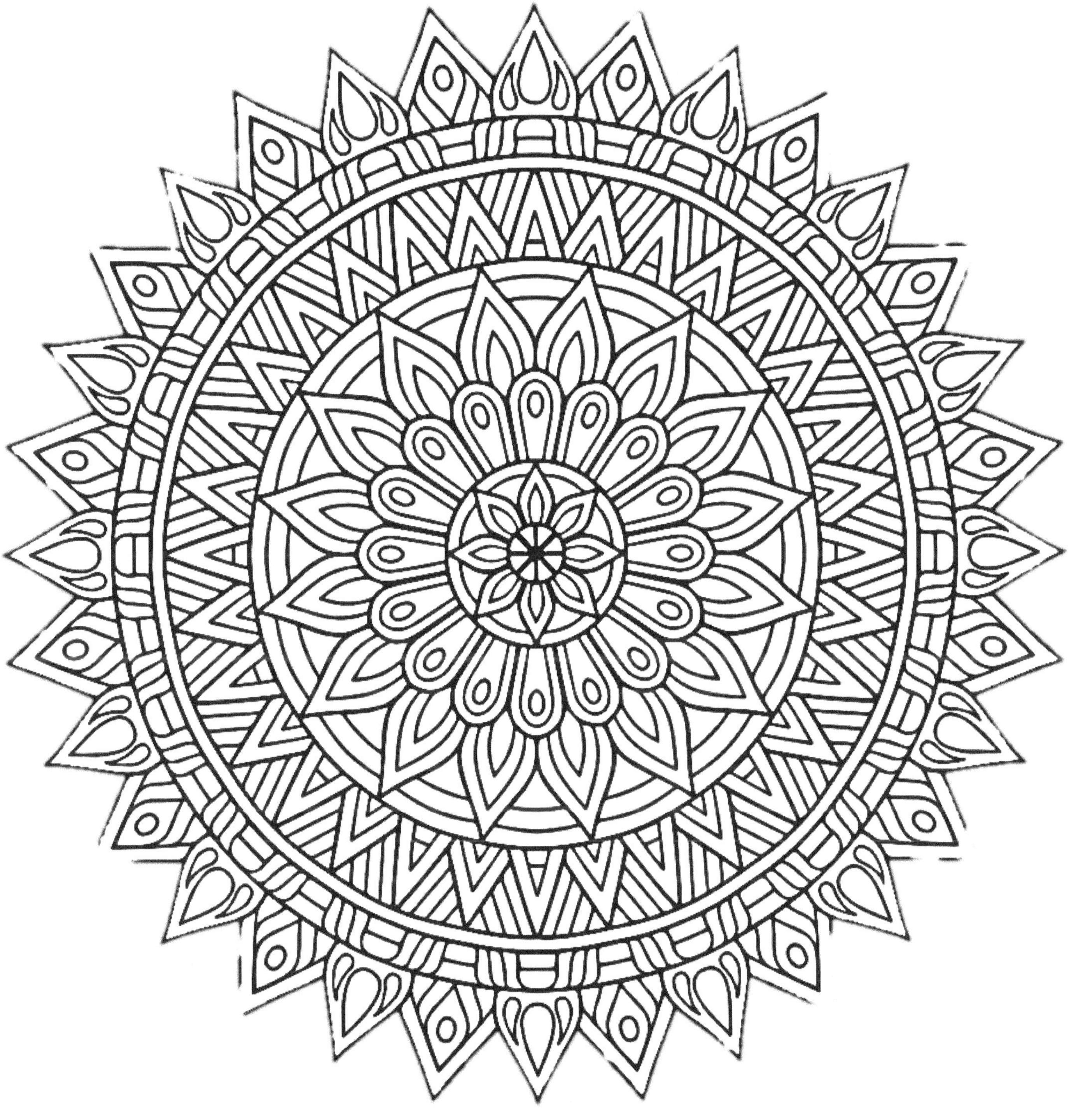

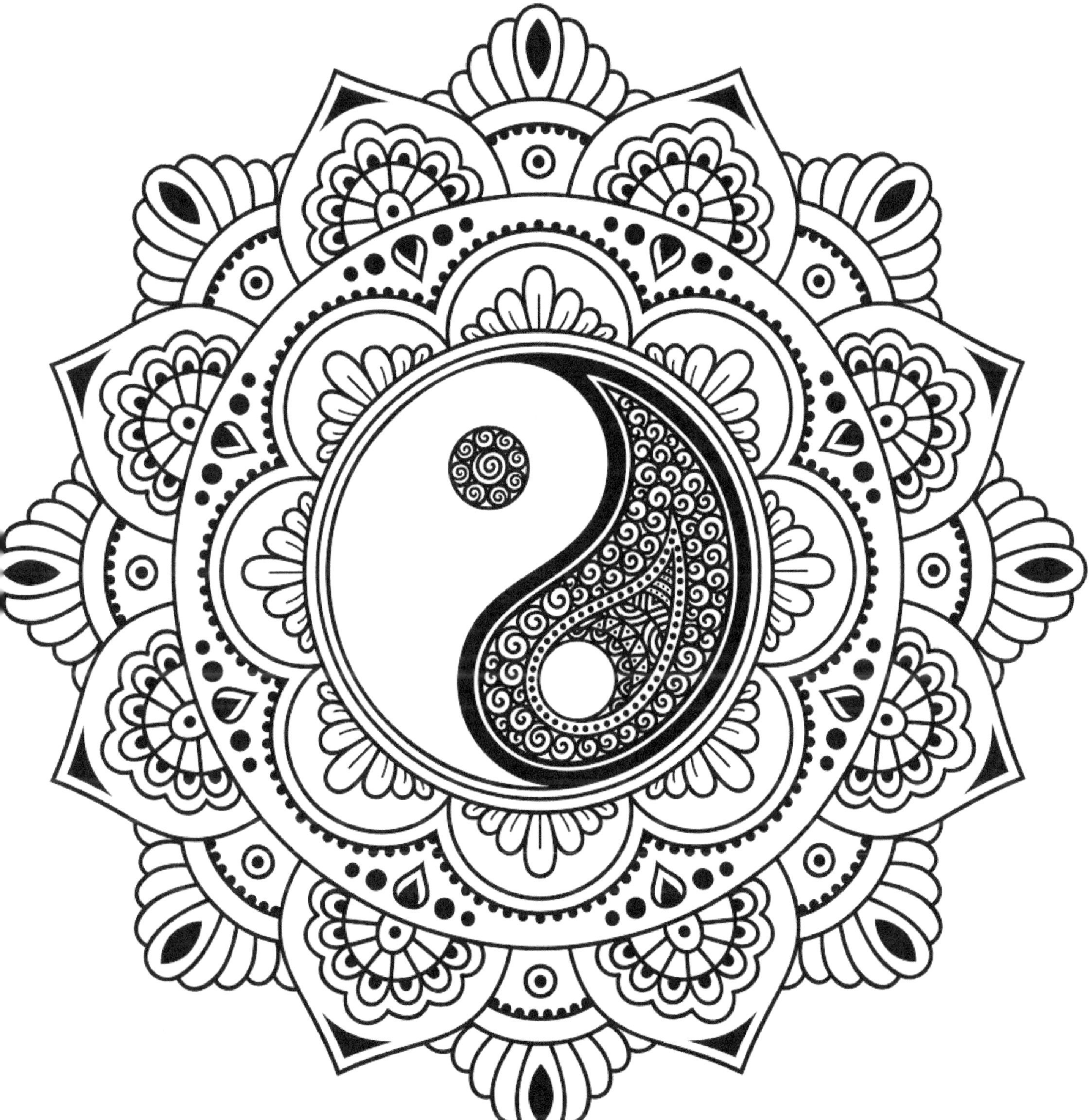

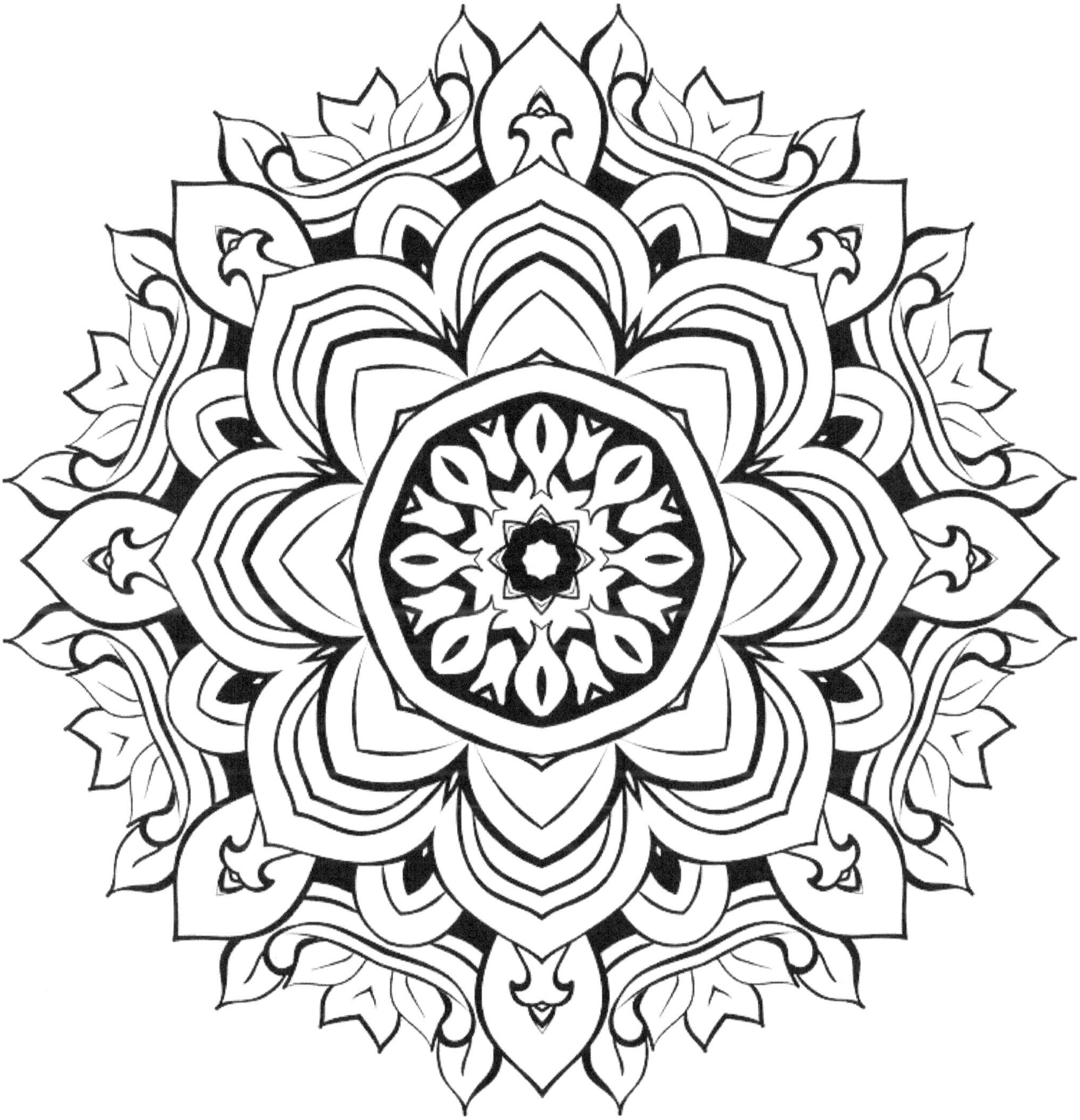

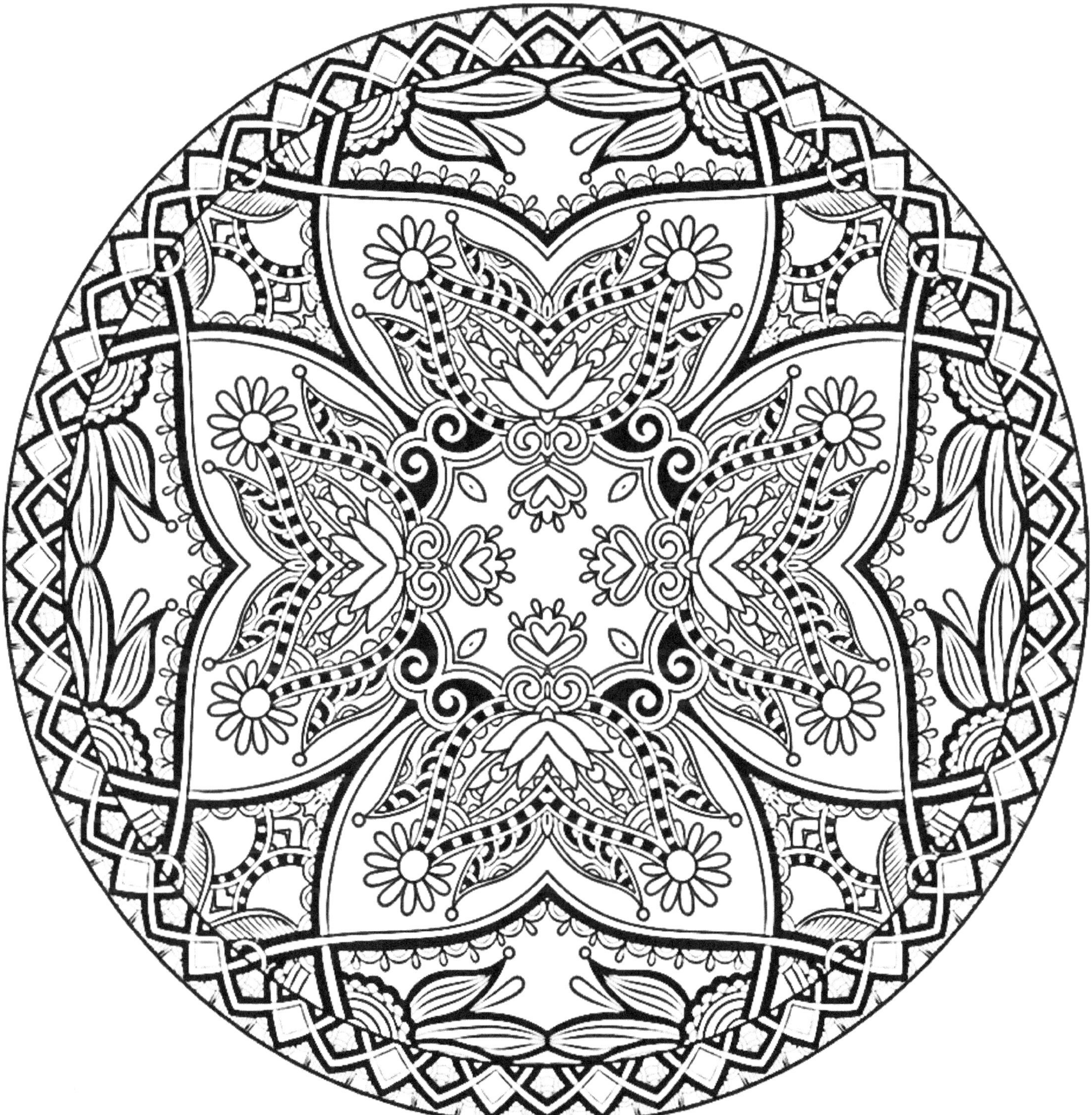

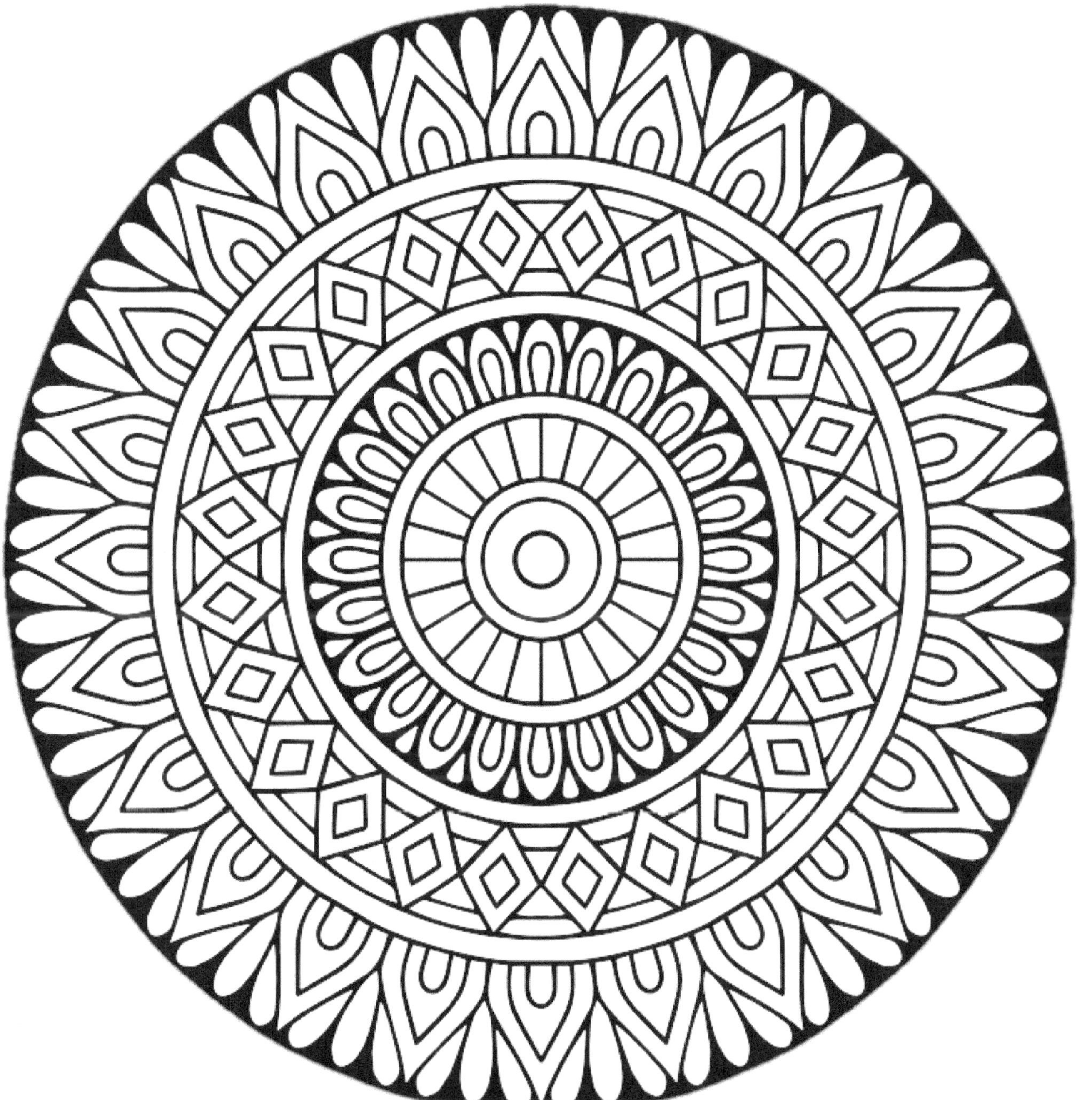

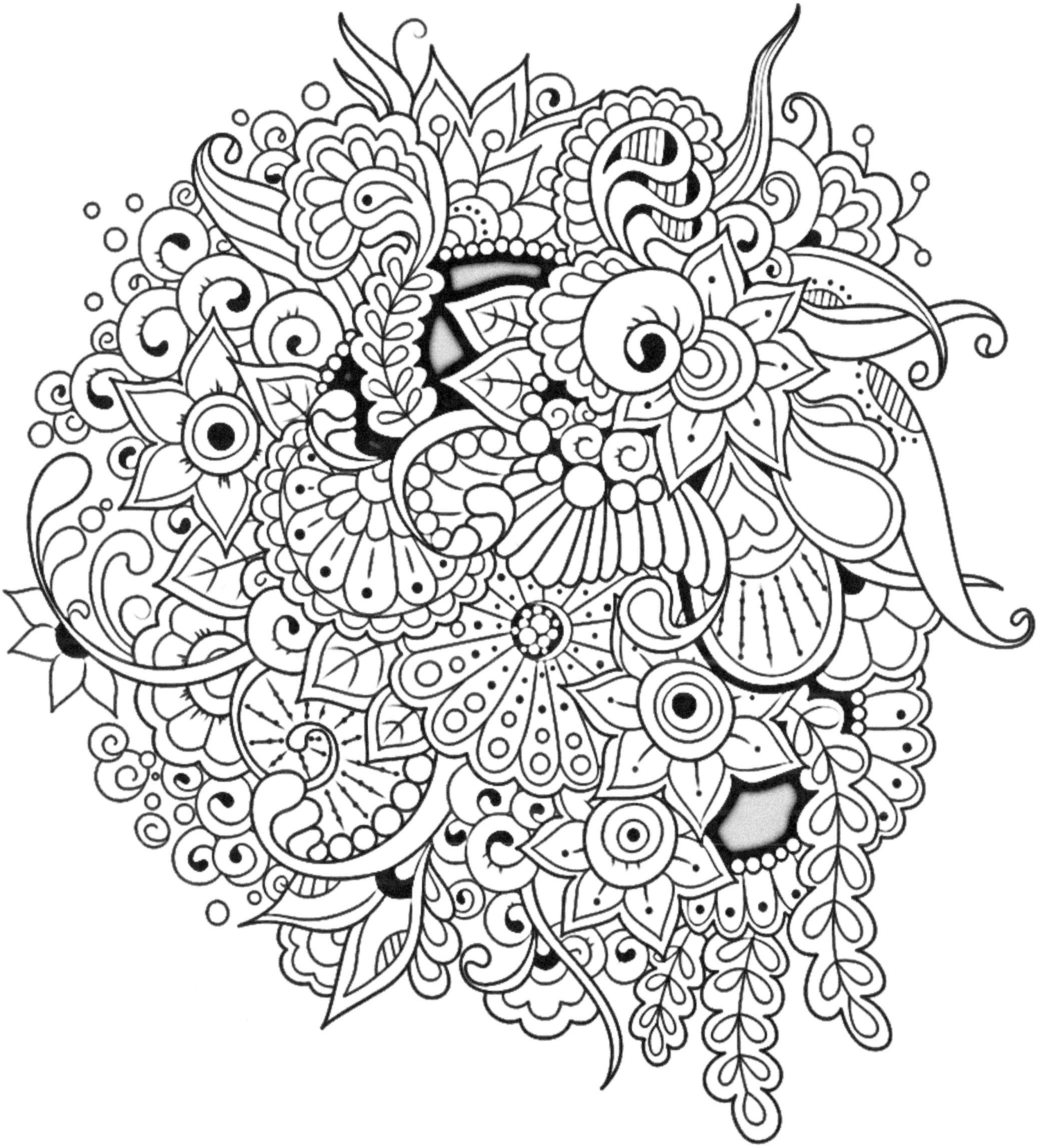

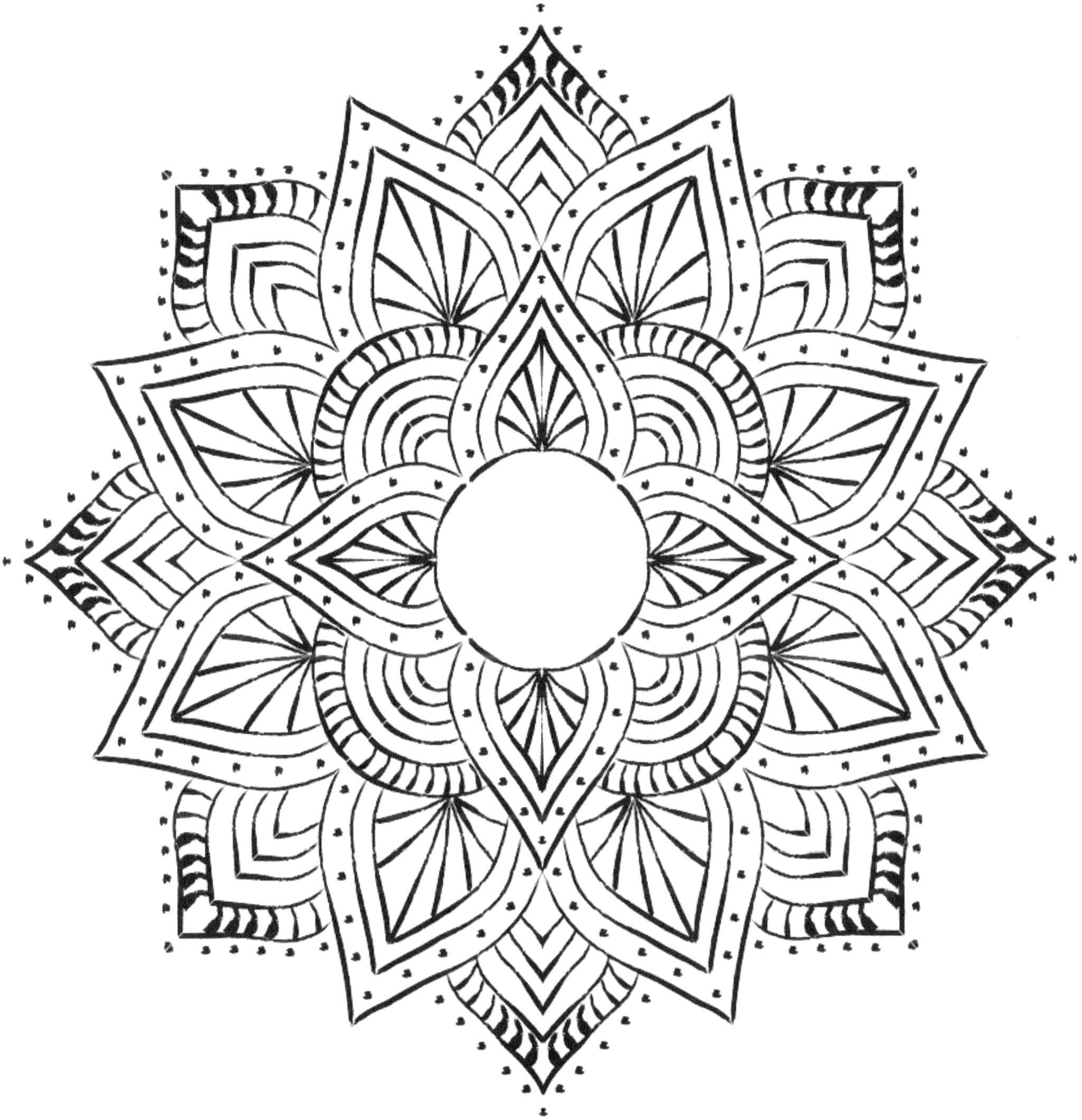

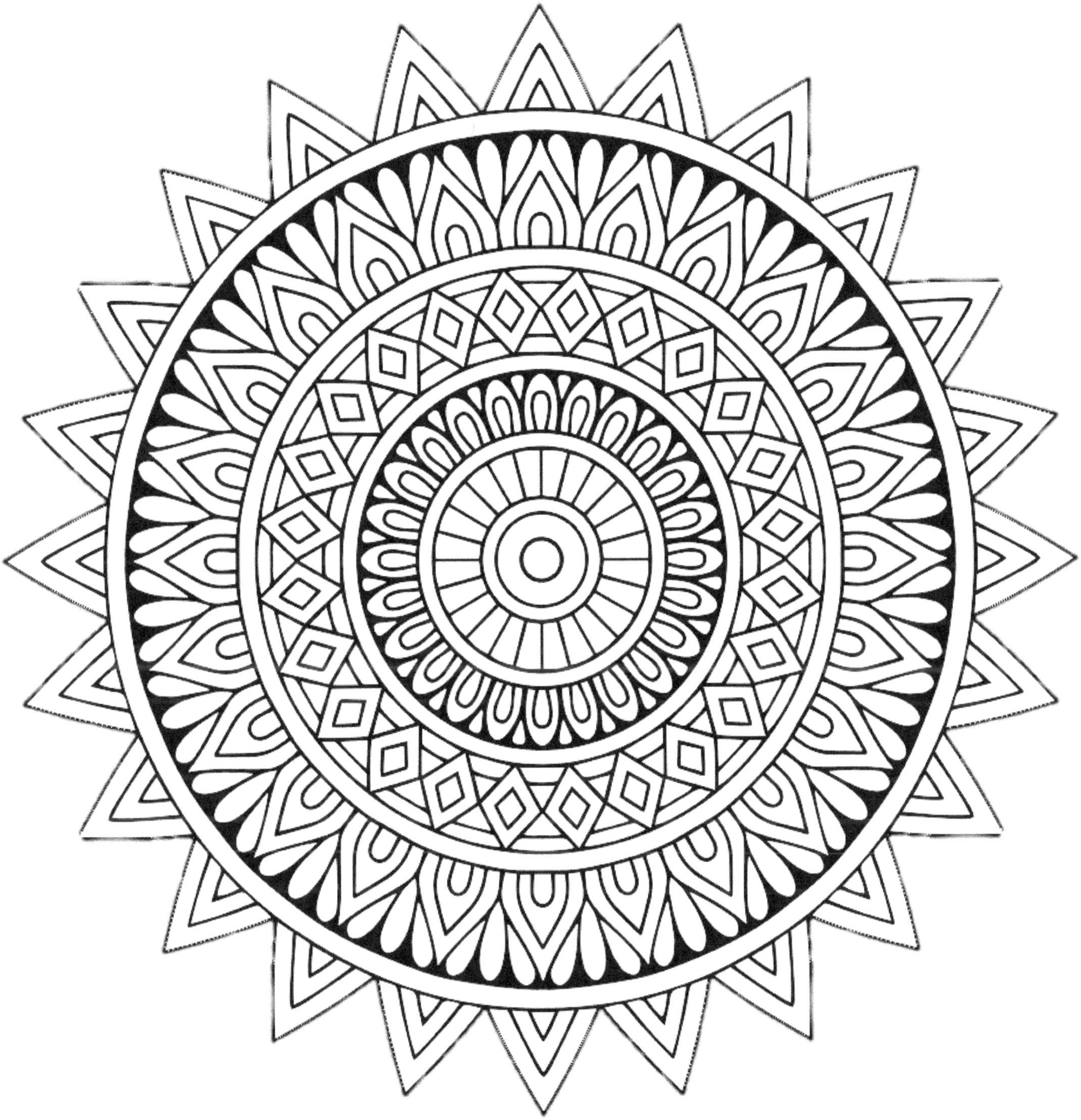

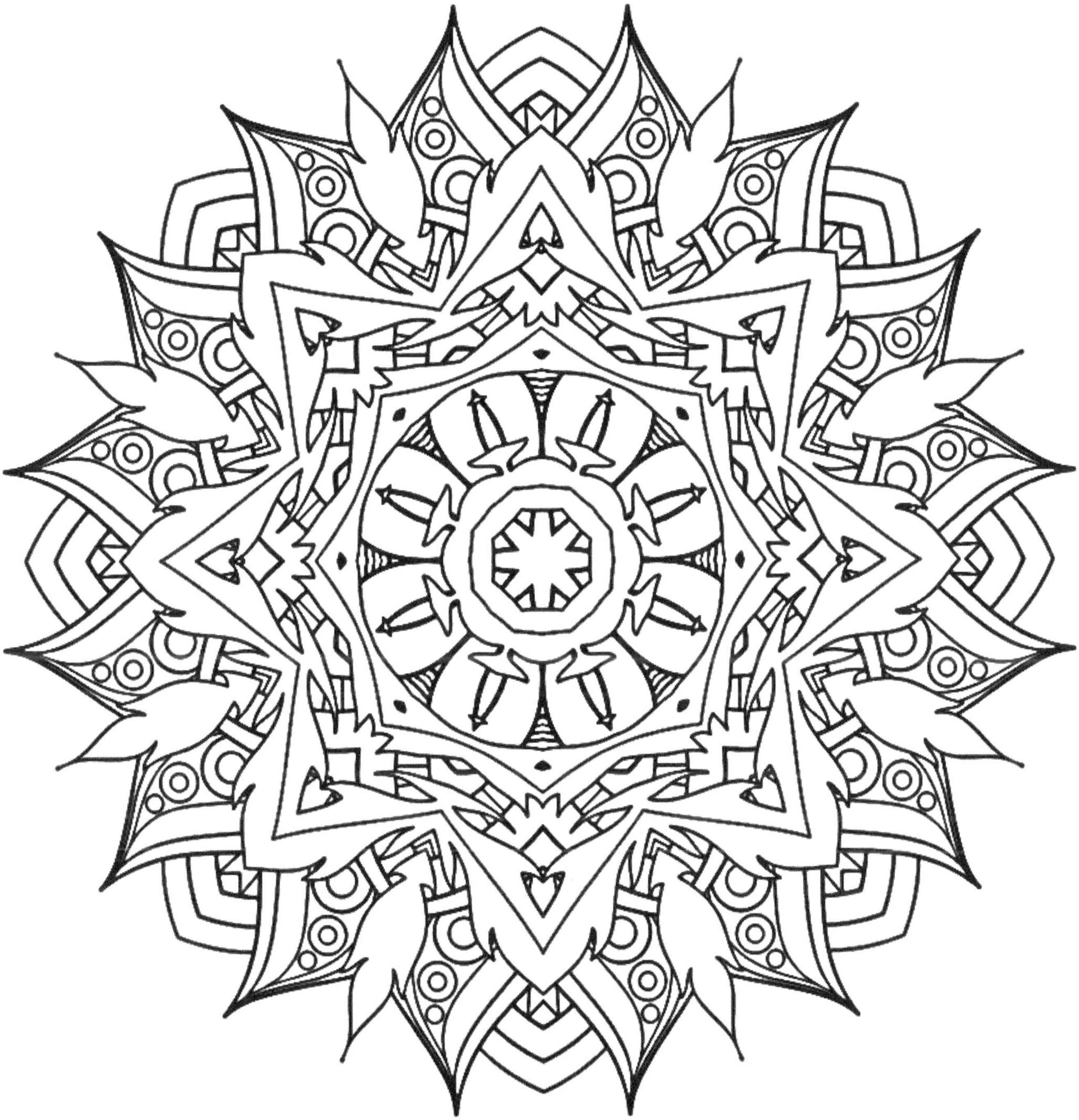

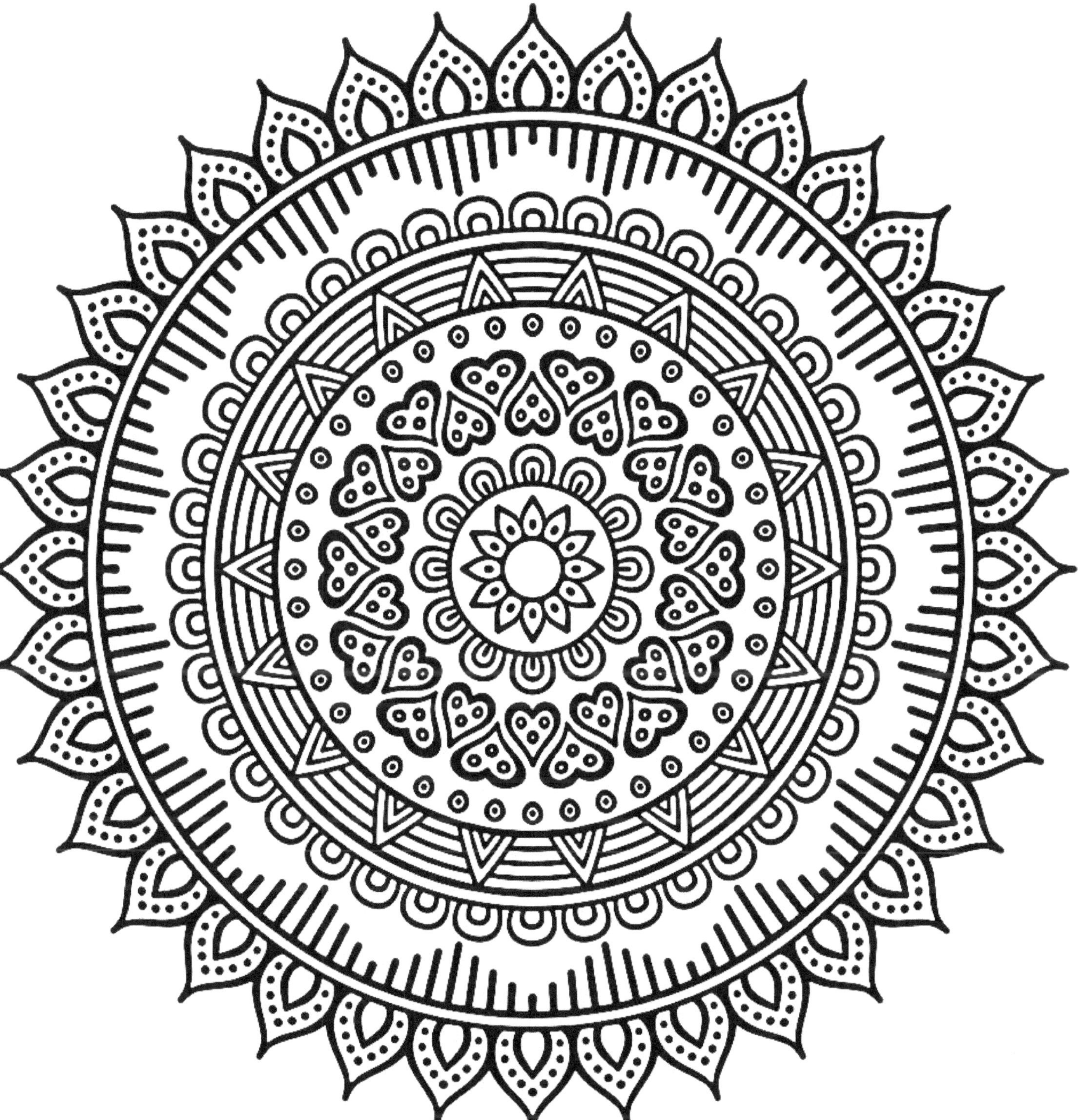

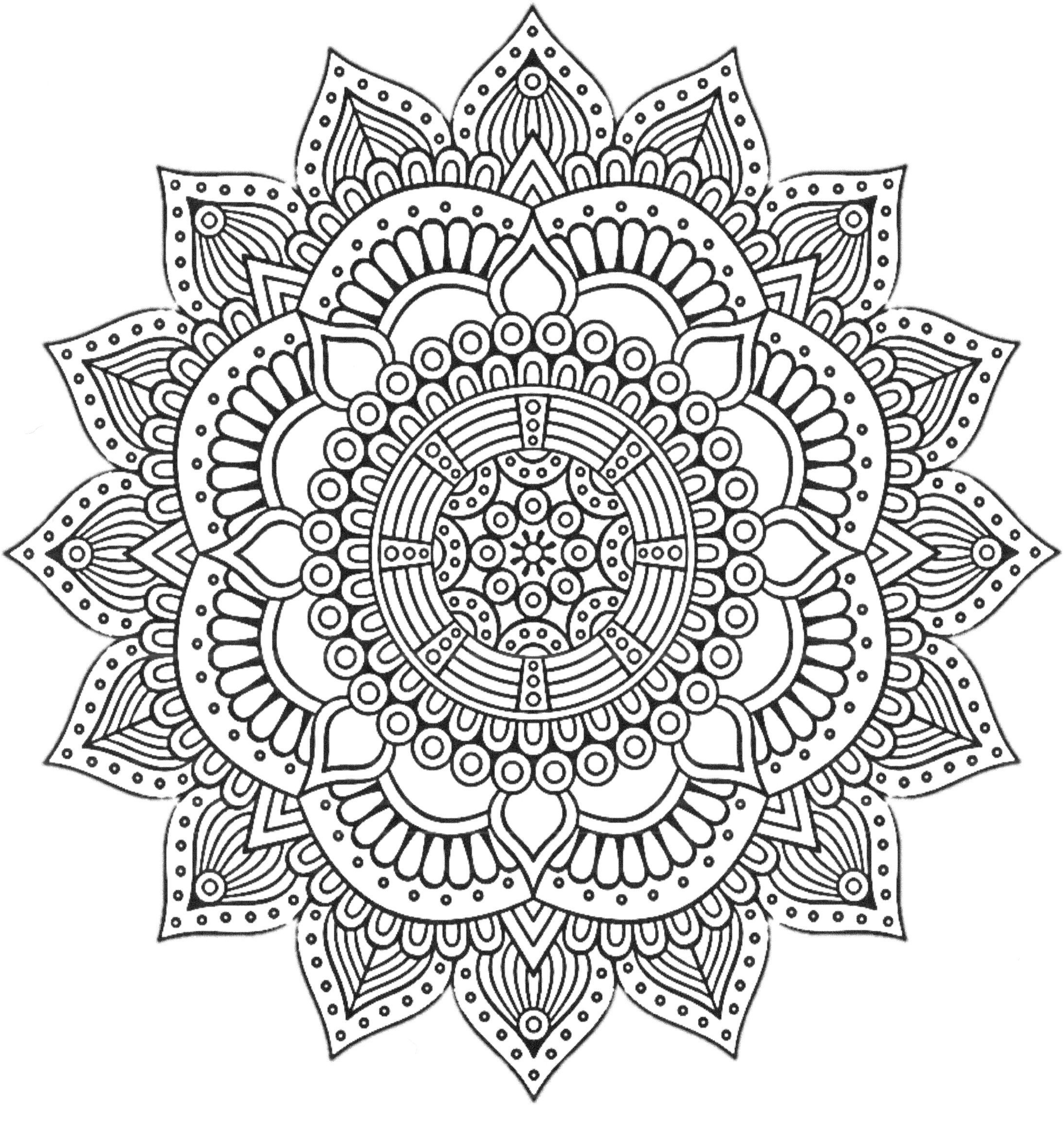

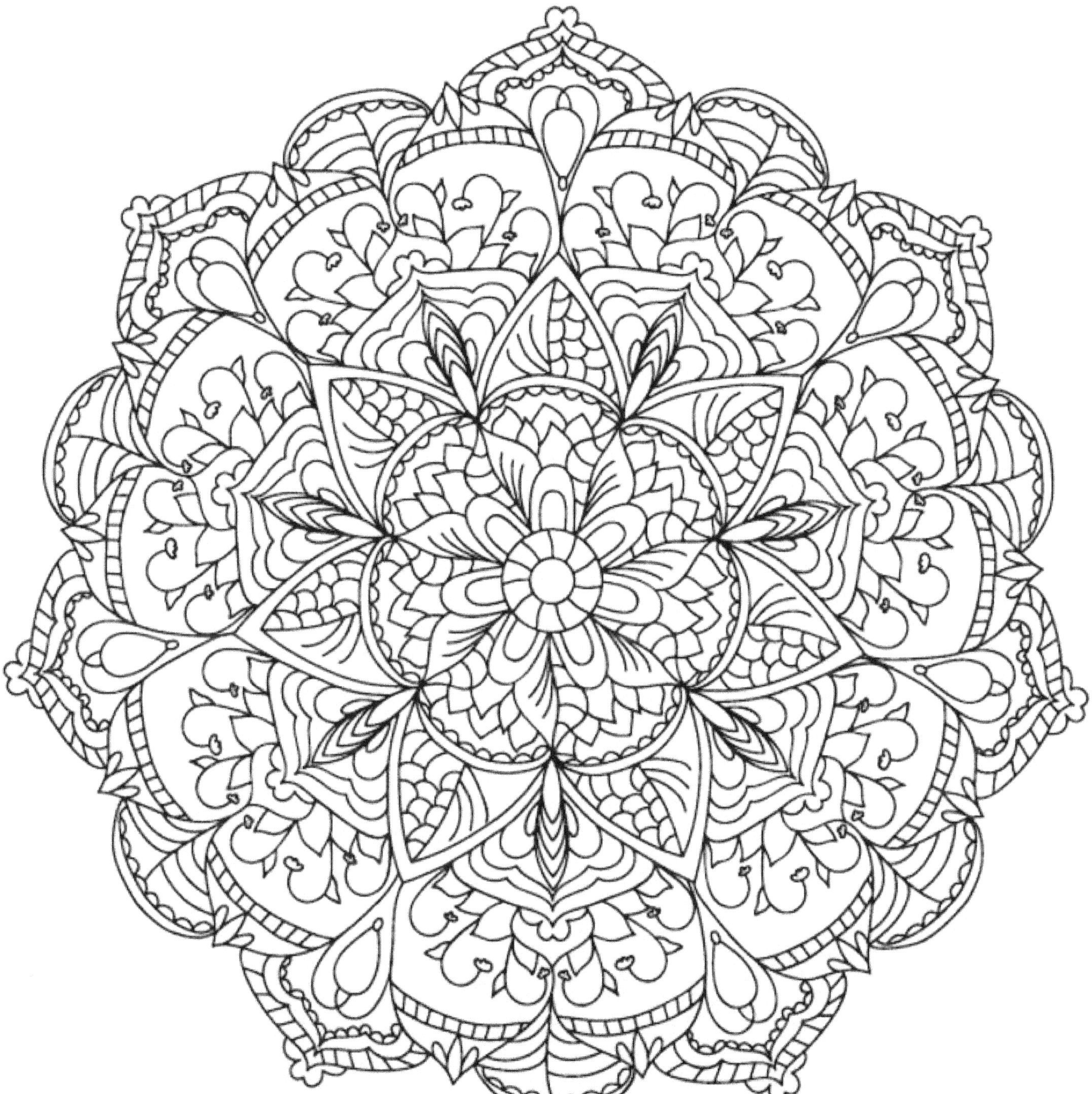

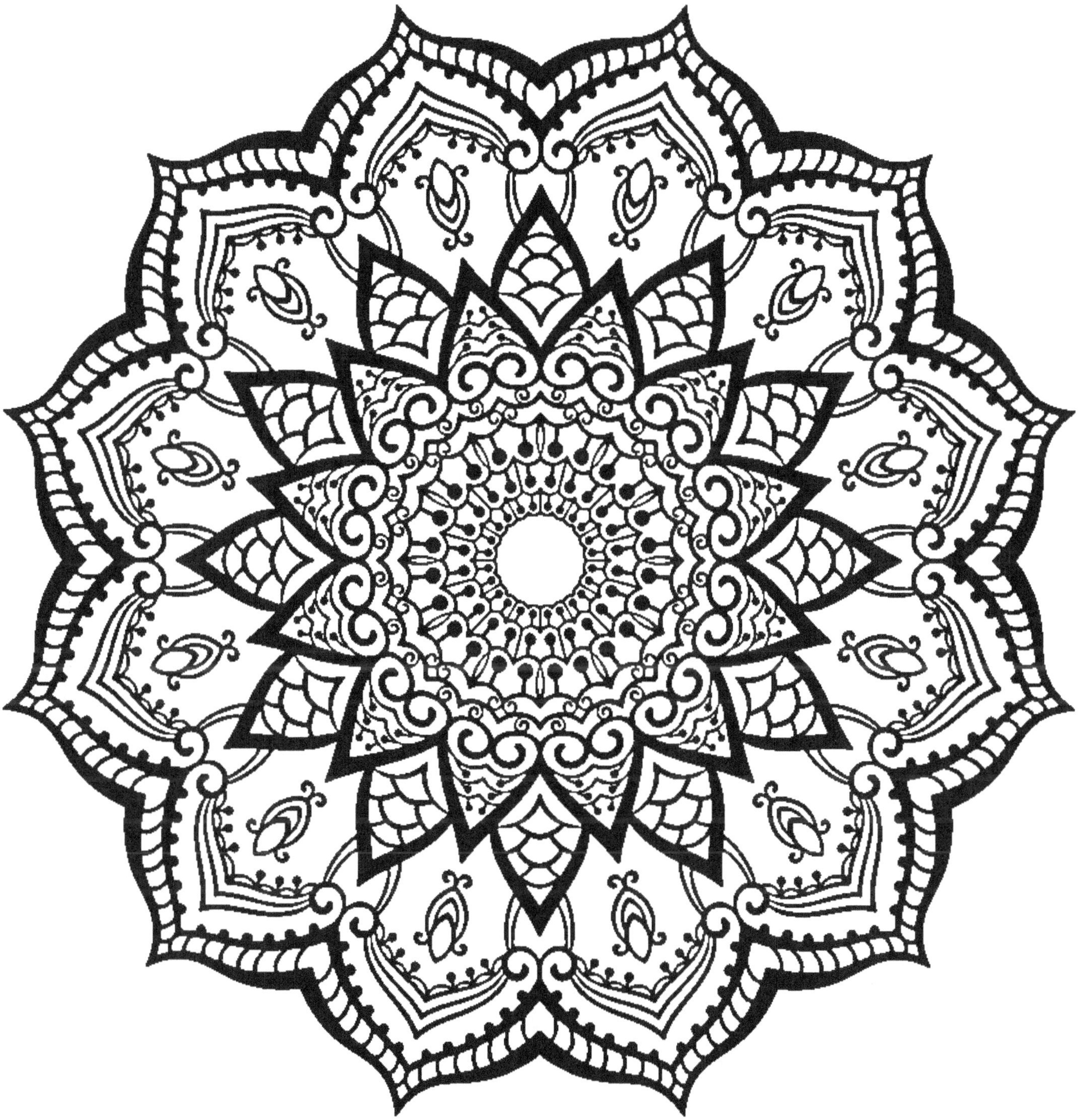

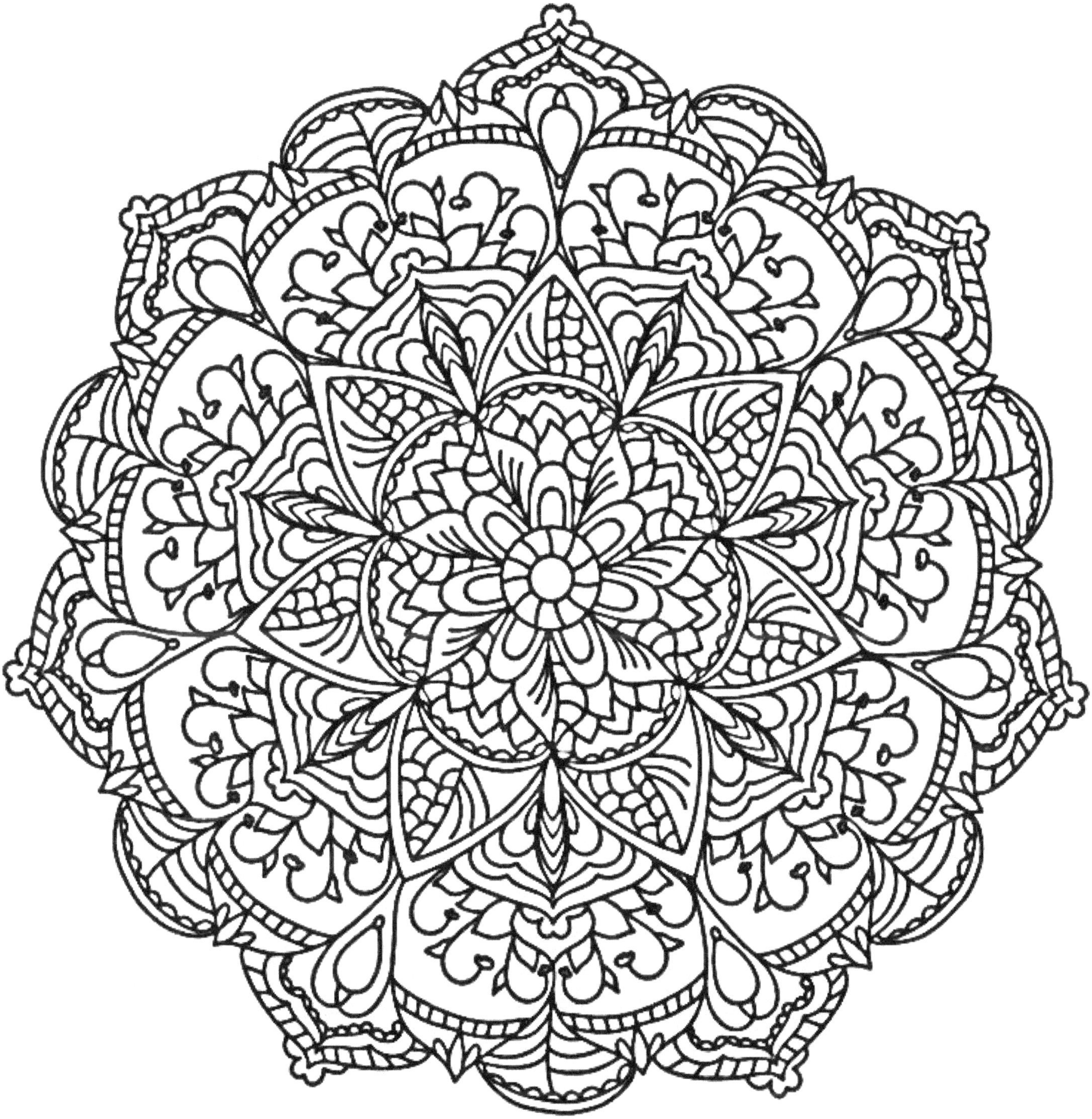

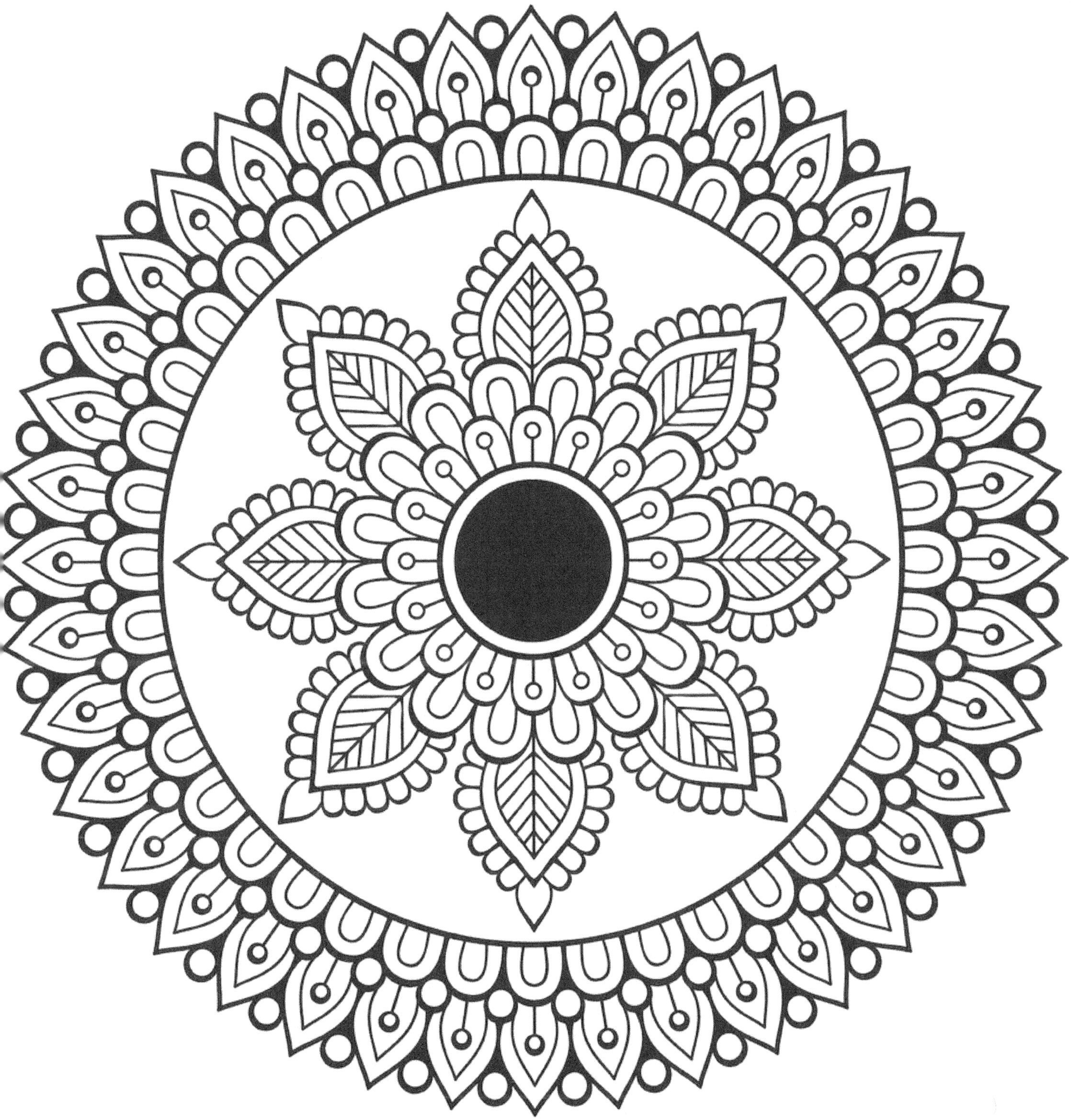

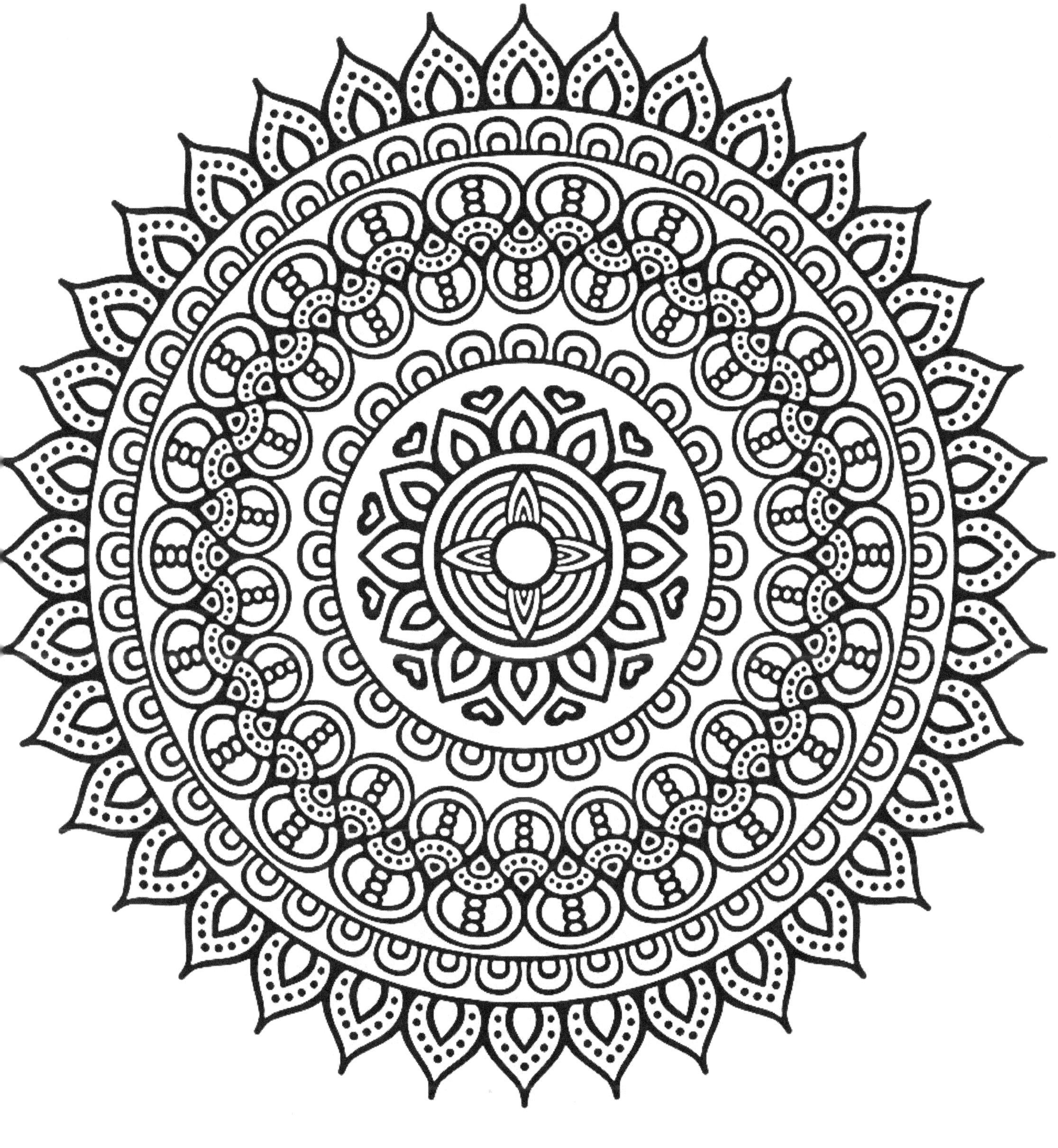

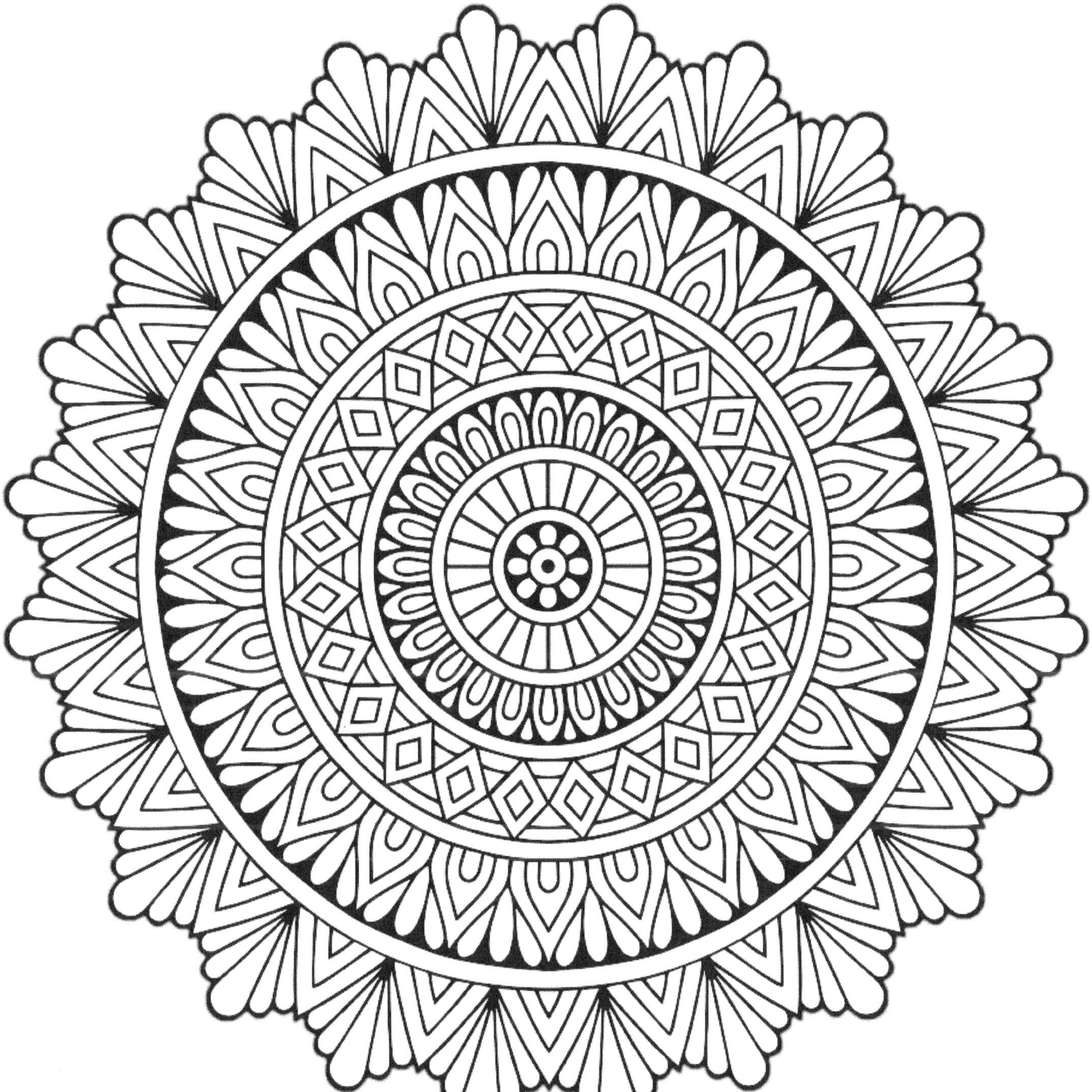

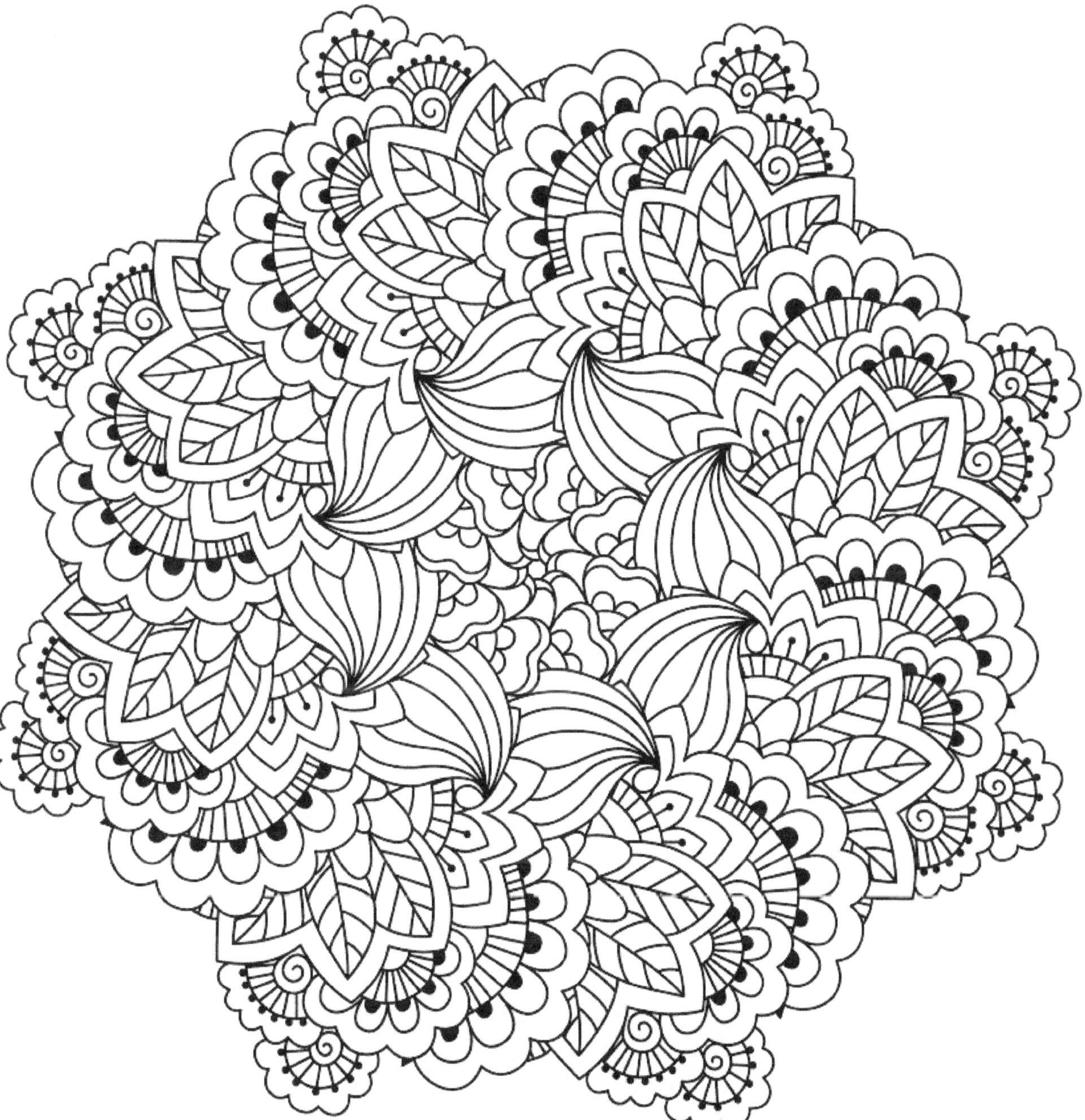

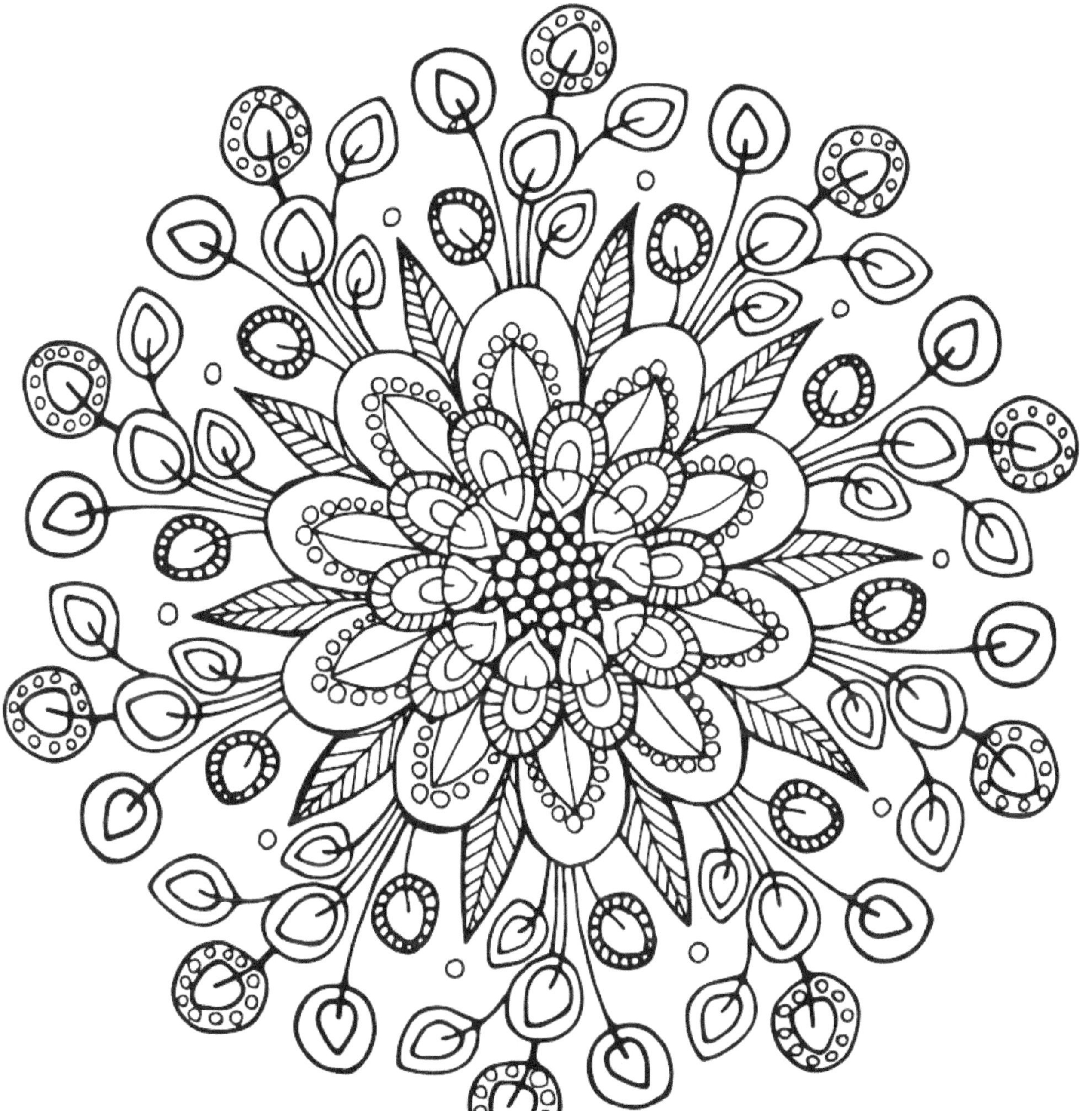

www.ingramcontent.com/pod-product-compliance
Lightning Source LLC
Chambersburg PA
CBHW082148230526
45467CB00043B/2407
* 9 7 8 1 7 1 7 5 3 4 1 4 9 *